Long May They Wave

Lee,   March 1, 2010

   I think you will enjoy
this story — you know many
of the characters!

Long May They Wave

The inside story of the banning
of the American flag after 9/11,
the hanging of dangling dildos,
& the punishment of a patriot
at the Boulder Public Library.

CHRISTOPHER J. POWER

 PICEA PRESS

Boulder, Colorado, USA

Printed in the USA

All original photography is by the author, unless otherwise
noted. Thanks to Joe Pezillo for his three photographs, and
to a friend who wishes to remain anonymous for photos of the
artwork and for the back cover photo of the author holding the
famous flag. Thanks also for the two line drawings produced by
my sister and artist, Elise Power of Pittsburgh, Pennsylvania.

Cover and Book Design: Scott Harmon

ISBN 10: 0-9785249-1-8
ISBN 13: 978-0-9785249-1-3
Library of Congress Control Number: 2006903543

Published by Picea Press
P.O. Box 401
Boulder, Colorado 80306
http://www.LongMayTheyWave.com

This book is printed on acid-free paper.

To my father, Arthur John Power,
who served his country in World War II,
and taught me many things,
including the wisdom to distinguish
between right and wrong.

— Contents —

— Acknowledgments —

When I found myself entangled in this incredible series of events, many friends and relatives would ask, "What happened?" It was not a simple answer, so I began to write it all down. That led to research, interviews, and the formation of a manuscript. The encouragement of those people and many others, followed by a lot of time and effort, resulted in Long May They Wave.

Thanks must first be given to all those who graciously granted permission to reprint their copyrighted material. They include Kenny Be for his cartoon that appeared in *Westword*, Pam Penfold of the Coloradan for a column by Paul Danish, Don Wrege for the lyrics of his two parody songs, and Mike Rosen and the *Rocky Mountain News* for permission to reprint his column.

Thanks also to the newspapers and journals that allowed me to quote their material, including Susan Deans of the Boulder *Daily Camera*, Joyce Anderson of the *Denver Post*, Ander Murane of the *Rocky Mountain News*, Robert Hershman of *American Libraries* and *Library Journal*, Patricia Calhoun of *Westword*, and Randy Miller of the *Colorado Daily*. Thanks also to the people who wrote letters to editors and allowed me to quote them. I also thank the owners of two online websites for their contributions, Richard MacLeod of *Darkendeavors.com* and David Max of *Huskerpedia.com*. Thanks also to Dominic Dezzutti of KBDI-TV in Denver and Jann Scott of Boulder Public Access Channel 54.

Every effort has been made to trace copyright holders and provide proper attribution, and the publisher will be happy to correct mistakes or omissions in future editions.

Thanks to former and current library staff members who contributed information and signed statements, and to Bob Rowan (the "Dildo Bandito"), artist Suzanne Walker, and former library volunteer Hazel Cowan for their consent to be interviewed. Thanks also to Carol Brey-Casiano, former president of the American Library Association for her opinions about flying the flag in public libraries. And I extend my thanks to everyone else mentioned who played a part in this story.

Thanks to Charlie Brennan, my stepbrother and professional reporter, for his journalistic advice, and to Andrew Biel of *BooksofDiscovery.com* for his advice about the publishing process. I also extend my heartfelt appreciation to Jody Berman of Berman Editorial, Boulder, Colorado for her editing and advice. Thanks also to the five different attorneys who reviewed and vetted the manuscript, and to the dozen or so reviewers, including former Colorado Governor Richard D. Lamm at the Center for Public Policy and Contemporary Issues at the University of Denver.

And finally, thanks to my family, friends and neighbors in Boulder, Colorado who had to endure this tale the first time around.

— Preface —

Where else but in the notoriously left-leaning town of Boulder, Colorado could a man lose his career and even his reputation for wanting to display the American flag in a public building?

After the attacks on the United States by al-Qaeda on September 11, 2001, many Americans responded with a simple display of patriotism and resolve: they hung an American flag. It conveyed a variety of powerful messages, from universal sympathy for the victims and their families, to the idea that we are still a united group of citizens, and that we will not be defeated by suicide bombers or anyone else. The flag became a patriotic symbol that brought Americans together during a time of great sorrow. Old Glory became cool again.

But in late October of that terrible year, one of the most baffling, and even anger-inducing news stories began to spread. The director of the public library in the university town of Boulder, Colorado had banned the display of an American flag. The local paper, the Boulder *Daily Camera*, reported that the director had turned down employee requests to hang a large flag from the glass entrance of the main library branch because, she said, "It could compromise our objectivity." Saying the library must maintain a politically neutral environment, she declared, "We have people of every faith and culture walking into this building, and we want everybody to feel welcome."

Coming so soon after the worst attack on U.S. soil since Pearl Harbor, the idea of the American flag being offensive to anyone came as a stunning declaration, an affront to even the most vaguely patriotic. Angry letters to the editor soon followed, along with picketers and protestors in front of the library doors. The Denver media picked up the story, and angry callers were discussing little else on drive-time talk radio programs. It made national news in several newspapers and on cable television. The library received some 5,000 emails of protest from across the country on the subject. A U.S. congressman even argued for a new law, televised on C-SPAN, for a denial of federal funds to such institutions that ban displays of patriotic symbols.

Just as the library director and city officials were generating spin to make the flag flap go away, the media took notice of a particularly controversial, and ill-timed, art exhibit at the Boulder Public Library having to do with battered women. Called *Hanging 'Em Out to Dry*, it featured a clothesline hung with twenty one brightly colored, full-sized, ceramic *penises*. They were not hidden in any way, but strung up near the picture window in the library's Canyon Gallery. The Denver TV news stations also noticed, not quite knowing how to show the very graphic exhibit on the air, and the controversy took a dramatic turn. The theme became, "It's offensive to some people to display an American flag in that library, but it's not offensive to display, well...those?"

The director quickly changed her story, saying that it was merely the size of the proposed flag that she found objectionable, an obvious inconsistency with her earlier statements. The news of the flag ban and the hanging dildos spread quickly, appearing in publications as diverse as the *Financial Times* of London and *Playboy*.

Nicknamed "the People's Republic" for Boulder's lingering reputation as an island of political correctness and ultra-liberal sensibilities in a mostly conservative state, the flag banning story became an example of Boulder-bashing at its finest for people in Denver and beyond. This scenic town where the foothills of the Rocky Mountains and the Great Plains meet seems to attract more than its share of publicity on the national news. A few recent examples include the unsolved murder case of JonBenét Ramsey; a football recruiting scandal at the university; laws passed declaring dog owners to be "pet guardians" and pigeons to be protected birds. My personal favorite image of Boulder from a more innocent time is that of the fictional home of Mork and Mindy.

More recently, a professor at the University of Colorado in Boulder named Ward Churchill has been in the news, also for offending people after 9/11. He wrote a paper portraying the World Trade Center victims as far from innocent, calling them "the little Eichmanns inhabiting the sterile sanctuary of the twin towers." His claim of Native American ancestry later came into question. But because of university tenure and the First Amendment, his paychecks from the State of Colorado seemed secure.

This is a sharp contrast to the Boulder Public Library flag/dildo story, which had a very different outcome. The facts behind what was *really* going on there were never told, until now. For you see, I was the library employee who suggested the American flag display to that library director in the first place. And I lost my government job.

The stories that appeared in the press at the time were strange enough, but the real story is much stranger, and more shocking. I believe there was a grave violation of the public trust in various Boulder government officials, and that the record needs to be set straight.

By wanting to hang a flag in the Boulder Public Library, I inadvertently hung myself, subjected to ostracism, demotion, and ultimately singled out for a layoff after fifteen years of employment on their administration staff.

I have debated for a long time about coming forward with this story, and it has not been an easy decision. As a somewhat shy person, I completely lack the bravado of Professor Churchill. But a large number of former staff, friends and relatives have encouraged me to tell this story. A current member of the library staff assured me that several people there will be "cheering me on."

Sharing the details of a former employer relationship is something I never would have considered doing, until this happened. But I am attempting to reclaim my reputation, and do not wish to be forever associated with the flag-hating, dildo-waving crowd in charge at the time. This story raises some serious issues about patriotism, censorship, the neutrality of government institutions such as public libraries, the excesses of political correctness, the growing problem of reverse gender discrimination, the destructive power of false rumors, and others. I won't pretend to have all the answers, but I believe that sometimes the best remedy for the stench of bad government conduct is a good airing. And, as we say in the library world, this story is "long overdue." It's time for me to stand up for our American flag, and the truth.

This is a tale of Boulder politics and personalities, the unchecked power of unelected officials, the skill and ease with which misleading information was distributed to the media to cover things up, and the unwarranted retaliation that occurred to me for "starting" the whole thing with my seemingly wholesome, patriotic and visually pleasing suggestion of putting an American flag in our public library after 9/11. Could this happen in America? Yes, indeed. So how should a person with a library background tell such a story? By writing a book, of course.

The story that follows is true. It is based on my first-hand experiences, interviews of witnesses, correspondence, public documents, and media reports. A list of the "cast of characters" appears in the back of the book for easy reference. Please keep in mind that I am not a professional reporter or writer, just a guy who was caught up in one of the most bizarre post-9/11 stories of them all.

Allow me to begin by introducing myself to you, how I came to Colorado and the Boulder Public Library, and the environment and personalities in place there before the flap over the American flag. Then the wacky, inside story of the flag ban and the dildos, and what happened afterward, will unfold.

Some dogs and their pet guardians walking below
the "Flatirons" in Boulder's Chautauqua Park

My Journey to Boulder and the Public Library

I was born in another mountainous state, in Charleston, West Virginia, and one of my earliest childhood memories was that of my mother taking us to the downtown public library. It was in an old, converted mansion with an upstairs children's room at the top of a long staircase. I was not yet old enough to read, so while my mother was helping my older siblings with book selections, I sat by myself and looked at the pictures in a book tiny enough to fit my hands. Then a woman who looked like my grandmother, who seemed to be very busy running the place, came over and said, "Would you like me to read *Peter Rabbit* to you?" It was the beloved children's librarian, Mrs. Brown. I sat in her lap as she read each page, making the illustrations come alive. I was amazed that those letters on each page made up an entire, wonderful story. I never forgot that extraordinary act of kindness, and it inspired me to learn to read as quickly as possible. And I suppose it was the start of my love of libraries as well.

Years later, that old library caught fire and burned to the ground, a traumatic event for the city and for me. In an uncommon example of intergovernmental cooperation, the county purchased the old post office building from the federal government, and converted it to a much larger library that is still in use, and largely unchanged, today. I remember frequently cutting some unchallenging classes at the nearby Catholic high school and making my way down Virginia Street to the library, where I could read whatever I pleased. I believe those daring escapes rounded out my education very nicely.

My introduction to the idea of patriotism was fairly typical. In my elementary school, we began each day with the Pledge of Allegiance to the American flag, always stumbling on the word, "indivisible." Summer vacations were spent on Cape Cod, Massachusetts, where the flag was prolifically displayed on Independence Day, with parades and concerts at the local band shell. My youth was about as red, white and blue as they come.

I began high school near the peak of the seemingly endless Vietnam War, and worried about eventually being drafted and sent there, as were my peers. The concepts of patriotism became muddled as the "older" people in colleges were protesting the war, and some were burning flags and draft cards. But the draft lottery ended in 1973, and the last man was inducted on June 30, 1973. I turned eighteen just thirteen days later.

After completing my undergraduate degree in biology at West Virginia University, I secured a wonderful job as a scientific research assistant at the Union Carbide Corporation in Tarrytown, New York, just north of New York City. But after three very productive years there engaged in some pioneering biotechnology research, the impending closure of the lab was announced.

Following the lead of two co-workers, I applied to the MBA program at New York University. NYU and Columbia were considered to be the best graduate business schools in the city, and to my astonishment, I was accepted. Now called the Leonard Stern School of Business, it is consistently ranked just slightly below the top ten U.S. graduate business schools in most surveys. The school accepts only 15 percent of applicants to the full-time program. Today the tuition is over $34,000 per year and median starting pay including bonuses is reported to be $140,000. And a recent business magazine ranked NYU as the MBA program "where your career prospects are brightest" and called it a "golden starting gate."[1] Sounds like a sure thing, right?

I was assured by the NYU career counselors that I would have no trouble finding a great job with my "technical" experience and their MBA, and that I should expect multiple offers. I had to commute from my home in Westport, Connecticut each day (passing Martha Stewart's house on the way to the train station back in the days when she was just a local caterer), putting in long hours on the trains, subways, and in classrooms. But the prospect of channeling my energies and ambitions into a fast track business career made it all worthwhile. I watched many of my classmates drop out because of the rigors, time requirements, or cost. But I wanted to be successful and was determined to survive it, and I did.

1. Michael V. Copeland, "An Insider's Guide to America's Top Business Schools," *Business 2.0*, September, 2004, 118.

I was filled with confidence and ambition, and ready to take on the business world of New York City.

But the rapidly declining economy disrupted my plans. The Federal Reserve's attempt to stop years of inflation by allowing interest rates to float triggered a crippling recession. The national unemployment rate reached 10.8 percent by the end of 1982, and the rate for white collar jobs in New York was much higher. Hard to imagine now, but the Dow fell to a mere 776 on August 18. Short term money market rates were approaching 20 percent. When I completed the MBA in the spring of 1982, I entered one of the worst job markets in the school's long history. I discovered that some on-campus recruiters were showing up only as a placeholder for better times, but had no openings. I worked hard for over a year to generate leads and interviews, using every trick in the books and then some. I was able to arrange more than fifty interviews on my own by writing persuasive letters, and came close to some fantastic jobs. But no offer. There were too many experienced, laid off workers out there. The business world was now obsessed by one's business experience, so a new graduate was at an impossible disadvantage. And the MBA was such a lofty, high profile degree in those days that companies would not hire them for lower-level jobs. The more time that passed since graduation, the tougher it became to get any employer's attention. The lack of experience was the main obstacle. I was stuck, and NYU's placement office and professors were no help at all after graduation.

I attended a memorable NYU commencement ceremony in Washington Square on a hot day in May, 1982. The MBA class seemed subdued, perhaps because of the shockingly poor job market. After all of the speeches, there was an eerily symbolic ending. A group of guys with long trumpets stood on top of the arch at the foot of Park Avenue, and blared out a tune as hundreds of purple and white balloons were released. Then the park's central fountain came to life, shooting a single jet of water high into the sky as the crowd cheered. A slight breeze caught it, pushed it slightly to the east, and the water came down and drenched the MBA section. People around us were laughing. We peeled off our wet gowns, tossed them into the appointed dumpster, and departed.

This carefully researched, sure-thing investment in the MBA degree was a complete bust, and remains my life's biggest disappointment and mistake. I have tried to put it behind me and move on, or as they might say, fuhgeddaboudit. But every year that I see those business school rankings and the high starting salaries, I get a pain in my gut. Perhaps one day I'll sell my MBA degree on eBay ("like new, never been used...").

I was almost able to take a career step backwards, receiving a good job offer in another state doing white-coat scientific research again, based on my Union Carbide experience. But when a company vice president found out, the offer was rescinded, because he said he "didn't want an MBA in the lab." The degree had become an albatross, banning me from science but not sufficient to gain acceptance into the business world. Meanwhile, the student loans were coming due. My parents were moving to Boulder in 1983, and I decided to follow them, not quite knowing what to expect.

I took to Boulder right away, particularly the sunshine and dry air. It still had a small-town feel in the early 1980's. I really felt as though we were far away from Connecticut when someone from South Dakota once told me that she was from "back east." I was fascinated by the Coors Classic bicycle stage races. My sister and I appeared, ever so briefly, in the Kevin Costner movie, "American Flyer" in a crowd scene on the Morgul-Bismark finish line, filmed during the real Coors Classic. I got a road bike of my own and regularly pedaled long distances to the north of Boulder and into the canyons. I took up cross country skate skiing at the nearby Eldora Ski Area, an ultra-aerobic activity that continues to this day. I also traveled to more distant places like Aspen and the red rock canyon country around Moab, Utah, a place so vast and endlessly fascinating; I fell in love with the American West. I also once participated in Boulder's Halloween "Mall Crawl" on the Pearl Street mall (a tradition now banned), where I was in a group of people in white clean room coveralls and white makeup, huddled in a giant cup, going as cottage cheese. We were the curds. One very drunk man asked me if we were a sperm bank.

But the full time job hunt always came first. After much searching in the Denver area, and several futile trips back to New York for more interviews, I landed a low-paid summer job working for a biotechnology lab in Boulder, where the research director had been a co-worker at Carbide in New York. I was willing to take anything. While working on routine plant tissue culture regeneration projects, I took on the difficult challenge of propagating sunflower tissues from single cells, a key step in the future bioengineering of the species. It had never been done before, and in that short amount of time, I discovered a breakthrough. The job was extended to almost a year. I was able to publish my results in the *Journal of Botany* (the editor kept calling me "Dr. Power"), and was later awarded a US patent. The Boulder lab soon closed, and I was once again jobless. I was beginning to think that every time I achieved something in life, punishment soon followed.

Keeping my MBA under wraps, and with my funds down to a level that could not even cover the following month's student loan payment, I took a temporary job at a savings bank in nearby Longmont for just seven dollars per hour, that extended to nearly a year. Ironically, the job involved the processing of student loan applications. The bank was eventually bailed out by the Resolution Trust Corporation. On one memorable day I stopped my car for a long, passing train on my way to a city park in a residential neighborhood to eat lunch. While reading a newspaper, I looked up to see the fast moving train start to kick up rocks, and then bounce on the twisting rails—it was derailing! I slammed my gearshift into reverse and stepped on the gas, just in time. A huge tank car of urea fertilizer rolled onto the exact spot where I had been waiting, broke open and spilled its contents into a giant pile. I could have been killed. I was shaken, but also convinced that this was a sign that it was time to get out of Longmont.

Fortunately, my introduction to the Boulder Public Library soon followed in 1988. It began, incredibly, with my response to a classified job ad in the local paper, for a "Project Assistant." Boulder voters had passed a fourteen million dollar bond issue and tax increase for a new library. The project manager for the library, Sally McVey, received over ninety applications, and interviewed twenty people. I was the first one interviewed, and got the offer many weeks later. I jumped at the chance.

I had used the Boulder Public Library regularly since moving to Colorado in my efforts to research companies and generate ideas for job leads. I never dreamed that I could end up actually working there. After a steady series of rejections from the corporate world for so many years, the security of a government job held a great deal of appeal.

Working in a rented office just off the downtown Pearl Street Mall, my job was to oversee the finances of this soon-to-be massive (at least for Boulder) new library building project, and to conduct the needed bids. I also assisted in the final stages of the architect selection process.

On my first or second day on the job, Sally took me over to the main library to meet its long-time director, Marcelee Gralapp (pronounced: MAR-sa-LEE GRAH-lup). Sally said, "To Marcelee, everyone on the planet is either your friend or your enemy. Marcelee's goal in life is to help her friends and conquer and defeat her enemies." I thought she was kidding. It was suggested that I try to get on her "good side" immediately.

We entered Marcelee's crowded office on the "bridge," the part of the old library that spanned Boulder Creek. It looked like a giant paper recycling bin, with mounds of paper and books everywhere, and a few staff people were seated within the clutter. In the corner was Marcelee, a large, formidable woman with a big, round hairdo featuring a gray stripe in the center. She was sunken low into a sofa instead of a regular chair. Her voice was booming, "Well, welcome!" She quickly put me at ease.

I had never worked for any kind of government before, so much of it was unfamiliar to me. Accounting concepts like encumbrances, carryovers, and appropriations were brand new. But I got to know people all over the organization quickly, and it was a great improvement over the bank. I also had health insurance for the first time since graduate school, a great relief. I kept my spending low so that I could meet the goal of paying off the student loans as quickly as possible. The loans for that seemingly worthless MBA degree had been my main source of worry for the previous seven years.

But I discovered a much larger, and more worthy goal. I was determined to get the most for those fourteen million dollars in bond funds without wasting a nickel. I remember feeling that, having paid taxes my entire life and never feeling as though I ever got much in return, I was now entrusted with spending that tax money from the good people of Boulder to build a library for them, one worthy of such a special town. I would not let my friends and neighbors down.

Sally and I, and her office assistant, John (who later moved to Nova Scotia to join a Buddhist meditation group), worked hard at coordinating multiple public meetings, preparing budgets and schedules, and drafting requests for proposals. It was a lot of work at a fast pace, and most of it was new to me, but I fell into it easily.

A very public debate came up about where to build the new library after the bond issue had been passed. The Boulder city council, with Marcelee the director in agreement, voted to build an entirely new building east of downtown, closer to the geographical center of Boulder, known as the Watts-Hardy Dairy site. Expanding the existing library presented several problems. There was inadequate room for the parking people wanted, and it sat squarely in the path of the inevitable, if extremely infrequent, flooding of Boulder Creek. But people in town were emotionally attached to the old place. Built in 1960 and expanded in 1974, many adults had fond memories of reading there as children, and everyone loved the view from the indoor bridge, looking down on the wild, rushing waters of tree-lined Boulder Creek each spring.

A group of citizens collected signatures, and put the building site to a vote. In the election of November, 1988, the downtown site won. Until that was decided, everything else was on hold, but then it was time to get moving. The important selection of the architect was the next step. I had no idea how difficult that would turn out to be.

Sally had placed ads in various architectural publications before I arrived, and nearly a hundred firms from across the country submitted their brochures and letters of interest, perhaps a reflection of the slow economy plus the appeal of a project in trendy Boulder. An early committee narrowed those down to about 25 or so before the process was put on hold by the site election.

A new architect selection committee was formed by the city manager to finish the selection process. Marcelee was on board, along with David Knapp, then the assistant city manager with oversight of the library, plus the city's planning director, the chief campus architect from the University of Colorado, and an architect from Denver. They narrowed the field to about 14 firms. It became obvious that none of the local firms had experience in designing large public libraries. Because of a slow economy and high bond interest rates, none had been built in the area in many years. But the out of state architects had no experience in dealing with Boulder's notoriously difficult development approval process. So it was suggested that the finalists form teams of local and national firms to provide the best of both worlds.

A short list of five such teams emerged as finalists. Without going into the details of what happened, I can say that Sally had serious concerns about how the process was handled, and shocked me by announcing that she was going to "vote with my feet" and resign. I was stunned, and tried hard to talk her out of that. But she was determined.

She first told City Manager James Piper and Dave Knapp, who each called back several times to plead with her to stay. Dave even offered the two of us an office in city hall, reporting directly to Dave instead of Marcelee. But no deal. Sally resigned the next day, and the local paper picked up the story. It appeared on the front page of the paper, second only to the news of Lucille Ball's death. Sally refused to give a reason for her resignation, other than to say that she and Marcelee had "management style differences." The reporter speculated that it was connected to the final selection of the local architect, known to be Marcelee's favorite.

One of the stranger expressions Marcelee used to use, to describe someone who got into trouble over politics or policy, was, "She really got her tit in a wringer!" Perhaps an old saying from her Kansas upbringing, it referred to the rollers of an old fashioned washing machine. The phrase was once used by Nixon's Attorney General John Mitchell about Martha Graham of the *Washington Post*. Now Sally had put a wringer directly in Marcelee's path by resigning.

I found out about a ridiculous rumor that spread throughout the library about Sally's resignation. Whenever facts were scarce, strange rumors from the staff would instantly fill the vacuum. They said that Sally really resigned because she was going to have the baby of a man in the planning department! It was, of course, totally untrue, and Sally had a big laugh when I told her about it. Years later, I would greet Sally by asking how she and her "love child" were getting along.

City Manager Piper was visibly shaken by Sally's resignation and the publicity that followed, and was almost certainly getting hammered with questions from his city council. A day later, I was asked to come to his conference room, where Dave Knapp and Marcelee were seated. I was certain that I was going to lose my job after only six months. Instead, Dave said that they were very impressed with my performance, and wanted me to move into Sally's job of project manager. He also added that the public controversy was still so strong that they wanted to fill the job quickly and move ahead without a lengthy search for her replacement. He said that he was impressed with my education and accomplishments, and was sure that I could do a good job. "You're a smart guy, you'll figure it out," he told me.

I was stunned. I really didn't know anything about managing a huge building project, but I also saw it as a great challenge. I was suspicious of Marcelee, as she probably was of me, since we barely knew each other at that point. I was hired by Sally, not Marcelee. It took about a year to win her trust on at least a basic level, and even to become friends. But I suddenly had a very important, and very public, job to do. My reputation was at stake.

The bid documents were completed, pre-bid meetings arranged, and a new approach was tried at my suggestion. For the first time, the city allowed me to prequalify the general contractor bidders. The purchasing rules called for the lowest bid of any company who chose to participate, but this project was too complex and important to struggle with an inadequate contractor. I came up with a procedure similar to one used at the university, and ended up with seven high quality firms. Then the selection was done strictly on bid prices. It worked out very well, and prequalificaton is now a routine method of bidding large building projects in the City of Boulder.

The bid process was delayed when a contractor trade group went to court for an injunction over a standard clause in the city's contract. That was my very first courtroom experience. The city prevailed, and the bidding went on. We ended up with one bid that fit our budget, Pinkard Construction of Lakewood, Colorado. We had a ground breaking ceremony under the plaza of the old south building on a sunny but cold day in November, 1990.

It seemed that everything that could go wrong did so, and then some. When the giant earth movers were excavating where the old parks department "Treehouse" building had been, a natural gas service line was broken, filling the giant pit with flammable gas on a windless morning. While the Pinkard superintendent was evacuating workers and calling the gas company (who had previously cleared the site of such live lines), it was my job to run to the surrounding buildings and get everyone out just in case, including the entire children's room at the old library. I remember standing next to the fire chief as the gas company crews were working on the broken line with their front end loaders, and as the chief saw one of the drivers smoking a cigarette. I cannot repeat his remarks for obvious reasons. But we survived the leak and pressed on.

We had an unexpected surprise while excavating for a new sewer line. The contractor noticed some glassy objects mixed in with the clay subsoil from a depth of over ten feet. They were glass bottles dating from the late 1800's, when Boulder was a mining and railroad town and this was the town dump. As the contractor volunteered to shake the earth from the backhoe, we would catch the bottles as they appeared, including a few from Boulder's Crystal Springs Brewing Company, long-gone local drug stores, liniments, perfumes, root beer extracts, and all shapes of ink bottles. Some had perfectly intact corks and paper labels that would fade before my eyes in seconds when exposed to air. I had never discovered buried treasure before, and it was exciting.

Pinkard began to pour concrete for the basement floor in just a few weeks. Meanwhile, I was in charge of a publicity campaign to keep the public informed, and also to raise interest in what was to come. I published newsletters, gave interviews to local reporters, held public meetings, and attended library commission and city council meetings. I also attended weekly contractor and architect meetings in the building site trailer, and kept track of hundreds of change orders. Moving was done in several phases, which required much planning and a lot of coordination meetings. But we got the job done.

I never forgot that this was a Boulder project. Just before Christmas, 1991, I came up with an idea. I suggested that we host a pre-holiday lunch for all of the two hundred or so workers involved in the construction effort, from the top managers to the sub-sub-contractors. This was not a waste of tax dollars; my theory was that if the workers knew how much we cared about their efforts, we would get a better building in return. Marcelee loved the concept. A Mexican food buffet was set up in the old Channel 8 studio. Workers came in and filled plates, looking a bit suspicious at first, but the event was a big success. Morale on the job site greatly improved over the following months.

In crafting the complicated capital budget, I discovered that the project was faced with paying over $100,000 in development excise tax to the city's general fund out of the library bond fund. Since the bond proceeds were specifically for library purposes, this didn't seem right to me. So I went over to city hall and looked up the details of that tax in the Boulder Revised Code book.

I found a potentially useful loophole. It was clearly written for private developers. It said that if the developer provides space for city use, such as a police station... or library, "that the city would otherwise have to provide," the excise tax would be deducted for that amount of space. Well, I was providing 100 percent library space. I checked with one of the attorneys, and after he stopped laughing, he agreed with me. I gave Marcelee the good news, thinking I had potentially saved a big chunk of money. I pointed out that it was very uncertain, and that we wouldn't know for sure if it had to be paid until the end of the project. She ordered me to take the excise tax out of the budget and put it elsewhere. But that worried me. What if we lose the argument and have to pay? She said they can't take it if it's already spent. I expressed fears of what would happen if we went over budget, and she downplayed that. They would still have to come up with the money, she told me.

Toward the end of the project, I gave notice to the people in public works that we were claiming the exemption to the excise tax. They said we had to pay it. The city attorneys changed their minds and agreed. Word of this leaked to a reporter at the *Daily Camera*, our local newspaper. Marcelee seemed obsessed with the source of the leak (a reaction to be repeated in the future), believing it to be from someone in the city manager's office. The story appeared the next day, and it got Marcelee into a lot of trouble. The reporter called me and I patiently tried to explain how this issue came about, trying to smooth over the controversy. The follow up story detailed my explanation of why the tax exemption was a reasonable request, and that took a lot of heat away from Marcelee. The next morning, at a staff meeting in the new children's library, she was filled with admiration about how I had defended her in the paper and possibly even saved her job. I had earned her loyalty.

I got a phone message from the construction superintendent one morning, informing me that "the guys dug up a skeleton" while digging into the north bank of Boulder Creek to prepare to pour concrete for a pedestrian bridge abutment. "What do you want to do about it?" I was asked. A forensic pathologist from the university was summoned, and he discovered that the bones were from several different people, not just one. The origin of the bones remained a mystery. The story made the Denver news that evening. I found out later that the joke spreading around the city was that the bones were the remains of the former city managers who Marcelee had done in. Not true, of course.

After the new library was complete, and as the final

renovation work on the old library was winding down, my workload was as great as ever. The list of problems that required correction was very long, and took nearly a year to complete. I pressed for a legal claim for some defects, and after much negotiation, received a $100,000 settlement from the insurance company to make repairs. Marcelee recognized that it was to her advantage to keep me on, to finish all these details that no one else would ever be able to do.

Despite the odds, the huge building project and branch improvements, at a total cost of more than fourteen million dollars, were completed under budget. The downtown library remains as one of my proudest achievements. My name appears as the project manager on the dedication plaque in the entrance (if it hasn't been ground off yet). That plaque also lists the names of the five different city managers who served over the course of that single building project (Piper, Knapp, deRaismes, Secrest, and Honey), a succession that made my job even more difficult as their priorities kept changing.

Back at the completed Boulder Public Library, the city council had approved some money for the library to write a long range "Master Plan" document. Marcelee liked my writing abilities and used most of the money to pay my salary and extend my job. When a long-time staffer in administration resigned, I picked up those hours and duties. After being one of the longest serving temporary employees in city history, I now had a permanent, full time job on the staff.

The Master Plan was an excellent experience to learn more about the history, philosophy and operation of libraries, and to ponder their future. I chose an approach suggested by the American Library Association where we examined the various "roles" that a library plays in its community. An extensive telephone survey was done before writing the plan, to get the opinions of library users and non-users. Support for the library was very strong, and basing the plan on their priorities and desires was effective at keeping the elected officials from exerting too much influence. It had a slow start with the 5-member Library Commission, however. It was to be their plan, but after months of meetings, it became clear to me that they had no clue how to proceed. So I told Marcelee that I was just going to write one, and then they would have a document they could chew on and edit. She agreed, and the approach worked perfectly.

The library was one of the last city departments to begin a master plan, yet the first to complete one. It was approved by the planning board and the city council with little debate. It was put on the library's website in 1996, quite likely the first public library to put such a plan on the still-new World Wide Web. Copies were offered for sale, and I sold nearly 100 of them from that web site. The Public Library Association in Chicago approached me about selling copies, and they purchased over three hundred of them to resell. That plan gave me much national exposure among the librarian professionals, and gave Boulder an increased national reputation as an innovative, cutting-edge library.

I took on several much more mundane duties there, like grant applications, telephone system management, working with our non-profit Boulder Public Library Foundation to fund improvements in the lights and sound system in the auditorium, dealing with lawsuits against the library, applying for grant money, and a wide variety of other tasks.

My relationship with Marcelee was very amicable in those years, and I got to know her very, very well. One of her management techniques I most admired was to hire the "smartest" people she could find for any job opening, not the most experienced or qualified on paper, and give them enough flexibility to gravitate toward the work they most enjoyed. This was never taught in business school. "Somehow all the work got done," she once said. I really had no experience in coordinating the development of a giant new library, but she believed in me, and I would not let her down. With a lot of fast learning and hard work, it came together just fine.

She took a great interest in the personal lives of her staff, with meetings tending to be as much about family, activities or problems as much as library business. When we learned that one of our library building architects shared the same birthday as my own, she would take both of us to lunch at Boulder's former European Café. The two of us would reciprocate on her birthday, of course. Marcelee and I shared an interest in gardening, so I would receive gift books every Christmas, which built into a sizeable collection. I was always trying to inject my humor into library discussions, and she seemed to like it, often laughing out loud at a volume that would carry for considerable distances. I was always coming up with ideas and innovations for the library, and she was consistently receptive to them. She was easy to like in many ways, and we established a relationship of cooperation and trust.

I became one of the few people on her staff who could openly discuss controversial issues, pointing out repercussions that had not occurred to her. After one instance where she changed her mind about a previous decision, she said that she counted on me to tell her what the right thing to do is, because "I don't see right from wrong the way other people do." I made a joke about how that was not in my job description. On another occasion, one of the senior librarians pulled me aside to inform me of something Marcelee said in a meeting of several people on her staff. She said Marcelee told the group that "Chris Power is the most honest person I know." I was stunned. Making another joke, I replied that she really needed to meet more people.

I enjoyed a fine relationship with most of the staff as well. With my background, I never really took on the traits of a bureaucrat, taking pleasure in parting the red tape whenever possible. The librarians noticed, one telling me, "You're the only person around here who ever gets things DONE!"

Marcelee was the most political person I had ever met. Her views were a source of fascination to me. She was extremely anti-war, for any reason. I once presented her with a hypothetical scenario, where an invading army was poised to move on Boulder to take over everything, and she was fine with that, believing that life would go on. She was anything but dull.

She had a "bull in a china shop" reputation in the city's organization, known for getting her way. But a former city manager once pointed out to me that she would always do such things to enrich and advance her library, and not for personal gain.

She could court the politicians skillfully. When the library first began to carry DVD's, she ordered a large assortment of opera discs for the still tiny DVD collection because a council member friendly to the library had an interest in them. She once told me she was a member of Mensa, which means she must have once scored in the upper 2 percent on an IQ test. She was indeed very smart, able to pick up on the strengths and weaknesses of just about everyone, and could think strategically. Despite her tough image, she could actually be very shy in public. While she could deal with council members very effectively in private, she could get very nervous and hard to understand when she appeared before them in public meetings and on television.

As Boulder's long time library director, she had some very good qualities. She never wanted to do anything to make people feel intimidated in the library or, as she said, unwelcome. While most libraries were hiring collection agencies to go after borrowers who never returned valuable books, she resisted such a move as too heavy-handed. She hated the idea of security gates that go off when an unchecked-out book passed through them, preferring to just accept a certain amount of loss, for which she took a lot of criticism. She had a very kind heart most of the time. I was once horrified to discover that her cluttered office was infested with field mice. She did not want to trap or poison them, explaining that they were such a frequent and loved subject of children's books. She once handed me one crawling in a plastic bag of candy, asking me to release it outdoors.

Her consideration of political correctness sometimes bordered on the absurd to me, but I usually found it amusing. Here's an example. As the person in charge of the indoor plant maintenance contract for the library, I had to order large quantities of blooming plants to display during the Christmas holidays. But she forbid me from ordering any red Poinsettias, concerned that someone might see them as "Christian" symbols, and therefore inappropriate. But she was OK with pink cyclamen, and after a few years I eventually talked her into pink and white poinsettias, and even some odd-looking red ones. And yet, she always insisted on ordering evergreen swags for the check out desks that had ribbons in the official colors of Kwanzaa. I always wondered if anyone ever recognized them as such, since African Americans are quite rare in Boulder.

Here is another incident where political correctness might have played a role. One of the library employees on the shelving staff, and member of a minority group, was suspected of stealing hundreds of the very best of the just-arrived books donated by kind-hearted Boulderites for the library, then selling them to used-book stores for cash. It had been going on for a long time, and the books were disappearing at an increasing rate. So, after many months of meetings with the attorneys, human resources and the library, the decision was finally made to catch the suspect in the act on video. Marcelee hated the very idea of video surveillance cameras, even after the theft of an expensive painting from her art gallery (That painting was quickly discovered to be in the possession of a homeless man in the city's Central Park). But the losses were just too great this time. So I was given the task of hiring a surveillance company to set up a hidden camera and recorder, which I did. It was like shooting fish in a barrel. I caught the man on the very first evening filling his backpack with books while looking over his shoulder at every moment. This continued for several more evenings. When confronted, he denied everything until he saw the tape, and then agreed to resign. Marcelee refused to press charges.

The next big project for me was the challenge of making our "bookdrop," or book return and processing room in the basement, more efficient. It was a nightmare. The number of returned items coming into that bookdrop peaked at 1,438,984 in 1993.[2] The patrons deposited their books in an opening on the outside wall, and magazines and media items (tapes and CD's) in another opening. The items slid down some corkscrew-like stainless steel chutes to the basement below, sometimes picking up sufficient speed to become airborne. The items landed on some large tables, where each item was

2. Christopher Power, *Boulder Public Library Master Plan 1995*, Chapter 2, 4.

picked up by hand, the barcode label scanned, and the book sorted onto a rolling cart or shelf. Books and media were sustaining a lot of damage from the chutes, and the staff was sustaining damage in the form of repetitive motion injuries. It was also hugely inefficient, with most items handled many times before they made it back to the shelves upstairs. My research found that the situation was pretty much the same in libraries everywhere. My new mission was clear, and I had Marcelee's support.

After spending a few years trying to be the first library in the country to install a robotic book return that was invented by a company in Sweden, I later switched to a startup company near Minneapolis called Tech Logic. Boulder Public Library became the fourth in the country to install their machine, which conveyed books to the basement undamaged, checked them in with barcode scanners, turned on the security tags, and sorted and placed each item on a cart, ready to roll upstairs for shelving. It was a huge leap in efficiency for a traditionally labor intensive lending library. It was during the installation and software debugging days of the Tech Logic bookdrop, and the tragic period just after 9/11, that the story of the flag flap began.

2

Main entrance to the Boulder Public Library

The American Flag Idea is Born

On September 11, 2001, I got up at 7:00 a.m. Mountain Time, turned on the television and began to prepare breakfast. The *Today Show* came on, with an image of smoke coming from the north Trade Center tower in New York, with Katie Couric speculating that an explosion may have started a fire. I couldn't believe it. I continued to watch, seeing the second plane collide as it happened. Then I saw images of people leaning from the top floors, then jumping. When the south building later imploded, I could watch no more. I decided to head for work, to keep busy, to do something.

When I arrived at the library, I noticed that there were many customers there who were unable to see this event unfold, and since we were in the information business, I decided to do something about that. I ran upstairs, asked Marcelee if I could put up signs directing people to the meeting room, and have one of the live cable news channels projected onto the big screen for people to watch. She thought it was a good idea, and approved. At least one hundred library patrons, and some staff, filed in and out to watch, mostly in silence, over the course of that morning. It was there that I saw the second tower fall. I went into my office, closed the door, and cried for several minutes.

Although I don't know anyone who died in that tragedy, I do have a connection to the Trade Center in my past. The NYU graduate business school was located one block south, on Trinity Place, back in 1980-82 when I attended classes there. My father, Arthur Power, was then working for an engineering firm on the 94th floor of the north tower (almost exactly where the first plane struck ten years later). I was in the Trade Center concourse frequently, using the ATM at Chase, or buying grad student essentials at the Duane Reed drug store (pens, paper, antacid…). I used to meet my father for lunch, usually at one of the bustling diners on Fulton Street, followed by a trip up to his office where we would talk, and I would enjoy the view looking east toward Brooklyn.

There was a World Trade Center experience that sticks vividly in my memory. I walked over from NYU on one gray winter day with light rain falling, folding my wet umbrella as I walked through the concourse to the north elevators. When I got to his company's lobby on 94, the lighting seemed different. As I approached Dad's office, I could see patches of direct sunlight here and there. I was up in blue sky and sunshine. From his window, I could see a lumpy layer of clouds about twenty stories down, and the only physical feature I could see was the very top mast of the Chrysler Building. I asked if we could sneak into the company boardroom on the north side for a look, which required special permission. After the OK, I went straight for the windows to see an amazing sight. Midtown Manhattan was covered in thick clouds, but the tallest structures were poking through and shining in the sun, including the Empire State, Citicorp's slanted top, and the very top of the George Washington Bridge. It was like being in an airplane, but there was no motion, no noise. It was a true, "If only I had a camera" moment that I shall never forget. I have since wondered if there were people in that room on 9/11, and if they saw that plane coming directly toward them.

My last visit to the World Trade Center was in 1999, when I stood "on line" for half price theater tickets on the plaza level of the south tower. While waiting for the TKTS booth to open, I chatted with people around me, nearly all of them from different Midwestern states. When one of them asked me if I knew much about New York, I replied that I went to grad school "right over there," pointing toward Trinity Place. The crowd was impressed, and one by one they asked me questions about getting someplace by subway, where certain attractions were, and so forth. I knew every answer, and for a brief moment, felt like a New York resident again. It was a nice feeling. I purchased my theatre tickets and walked out the door onto the windy plaza, past the spherical sculpture by Fritz Koenig, never imagining that it would be my last visit. I have been to Ground Zero three times since 9/11, not quite comprehending that something so huge and so permanent was simply no longer there.

A few weeks after the attacks, a plain envelope from NYU arrived by mail, containing a single page letter with the names of about thirty business school alumni who were reported as missing in the Trade Center attack. There was one name from the MBA class of '82, but it was someone I never knew. That was a chilling letter, and made me think that if things had gone differently after graduation, I might have been in there with them.

Back at the Boulder library on 9/11, an argument came up that afternoon over the news broadcasts that I had shown in the meeting room. Priscilla Hudson, the main branch manager, approached me and said, in an angry tone, that she was upset that I had not cleared the broadcast event with her first. I found out later that someone on her staff had the same idea that morning, and she had said no. This was ridiculous. Thousands of Americans had just been killed, more planes could be on the way, and this is what she is worried about? I just pointed out that her boss, Marcelee, approved, and she backed off. In a meeting with the Library Commission a few weeks later, a commissioner asked what the library had done in response to the events of 9/11, and someone in attendance told me that Priscilla or Marcelee boasted that we had turned on the news and invited patrons to watch the event live.

In the weeks that followed, everyone at the library seemed to be going through their days with the same mix of emotions as the rest of the country, like shock, anger, and fear of what will happen next.

In the extensive television coverage, I noticed that people and businesses in New York had adopted the American Flag as a symbol of solidarity and resolve, and flag displays were appearing just about everywhere. I also noticed that there weren't very many in Boulder, and in my own mind, the idea of displaying a flag in the library was born. But where would it go?

The downtown branch features a large, glass dome

over the entrance, supported by an aluminum "space frame" inside that resembles an assembly of giant tinker-toys. It is illuminated at night with a series of halogen lamps. The architectural idea was to draw attention to the main entrance in a very spread out building that spanned two city blocks. When it was completed, most people assumed that it was built to resemble one of the sandstone "flatiron" rock formations on the west side of Boulder. Geometrically, one of the architects called it a "truncated, skewed coneoid," which most of us shortened to "The Coneoid." When the building was being designed, Marcelee made sure that there was a generous allowance in the construction contract to place some kind of mobile art work inside the coneoid. This was done so that she could choose the art herself without dealing with the arts commission or getting pressure to use a local artist. It was cleverly called an "architectural element" instead of a sculpture or art. As it turned out, the budget was so stretched at the end of the project after hundreds of change orders that the allowance had to be spent on other things, and no hanging art was ever installed in the coneoid. $62,090 was backed out of the general contract for giving up that allowance.[3]

So it came to me: what a perfect place to display an American Flag! It was time to act, and quickly.

Marcelee was busy in meetings that week, and I was occupied with the Tech Logic bookdrop crew in the basement, so I sent her the initial idea in the following email, which I saved. This is the memo that started it all. Note the mention of possible controversy, which was only meant to be mildly amusing.

3. Main Library construction documents, Construction change authorization 133, Change order request 168.

From: Chris Power
To: Marcelee Gralapp
Date: Wed. Oct 3, 2001 11:06 a.m.
Subject: Old Glory??

Marcelee,

I keep missing you, or else someone else has been in your office. I had an idea that has a short shelf life, so here it is.

I'd like to have us hang a large US flag in the upper reaches of the coneoid, with some of the halogen space frame lights turned around to light it up. It would look very cool to people walking or even driving by, now that the days are getting shorter. I believe it would be a very timely and powerful symbol for our public library to display a flag in this building, and the coneoid seems like a perfect spot.

Mark [*Koschade, head of Library Maintenance*] has agreed to help install it with the electric lift. There are just two problems, paying for a big flag, and finding one for sale. I called all over Denver yesterday, and NO ONE has any flags in stock. Most are taking names for a waitlist. I took some measurements yesterday, and the minimum size I would recommend is 10' × 15', which runs around $250. A company in Westminster said the larger sizes are not in such great demand, so we stand a good chance of getting one in a few weeks if we get on their list now.

I'd be really, really surprised if this were to stir up any controversy—who could possibly take offense, other than any pro-Taliban Boulderites (I'm sure there must be a few). Let me know what you think!

Chris

Oh, that next to last sentence turned out to be very prophetic! My sales pitch must have worked, as she replied only thirteen minutes later:

From: Marcelee Gralapp
To: Chris Power
Date: Wed. Oct 3, 2001 11:19 a.m.
Subject: Re: Old Glory??

I'm usually not hot on this sort of thing—however these are not "usually" times, so go ahead.

She approved. I remember thinking, as I read this, that it was kind of an strange answer, perhaps as if the horrific events of 9/11 freed her from the usual concern of starting a public controversy. But the key phrase was "go ahead." I wrapped it up as follows:

From: Chris Power
To: Marcelee Gralapp
Date: Wed. Oct. 3, 2001 11:31 a.m.
Subject: Re: Old Glory??

Great! I'll get on the waitlist for a flag. Thanks.

This was now a new priority on my list of things to do at the library, and my excitement was growing. I now had something positive that I could do for the people of Boulder as a response to the horrors of 9/11. Rather than getting on a local waitlist, I checked for flags on eBay. As expected, there were quite a few to choose from, even in that 10' × 15' size. I settled on one from a seller near Seattle who offered it with a "Buy It Now" option for $250 plus shipping. I remember showing the eBay pages to Marcelee, which included a photo of the big flag with a person standing next to it, holding it up. She could see how large it was.

She approved of the expenditure of city funds for the flag purchase. I used my eBay identity to buy it, and was quickly reimbursed by the library. In other words, the city taxpayers paid for the big flag—it was not mine. Delivery would take about a week.

I also quickly realized that this flag would be very visible to thousands of people, so it had to be hung properly, without sags or wrinkles, or movement from the ventilation ducts. I met with Mark in Maintenance, and I spoke to his two custodians who are both naturalized citizens, Sohka from Cambodia and Majid from Morocco, who seemed very excited about the flag idea. All agreed to cooperate in hanging it up in the coneoid, somehow. We were all new to this. But Mark made a good point. He would only do this if I made sure we followed the proper protocols for hanging a flag. None of us knew the specifics of flag etiquette, so I agreed to check with our reference librarians, which I did. When I went upstairs to ask them, a librarian produced a book with all the illustrated flag display rules. It explained that hanging an American flag vertically is fine, as long as the star field is on the left when viewed. It was not as clear what happens if it can be seen from both sides, so we planned to remain flexible about facing the flag east or north, agreeing to try it both ways. If there were complaints about how we displayed it, we would have these guidelines as our defense.

There were three or four reference librarians at the desk that day, and they all seemed quite enthusiastic about the flag idea. I thought this was going to be a great thing to do for the library, and for the people of Boulder.

The rest of my week was spent mainly in the library basement, working with the Tech Logic people from Minnesota on the new bookdrop machine. On Thursday, one day after her flag display approval, I went by

Marcelee's office after 5:00 p.m. to see if she was still there, and there she was, typing on her computer. The rest of the Administration office was deserted. I knocked, was invited in, and I sat across from her as I delivered an update on the bookdrop progress.

Changing subjects, I proudly told her that the flag should arrive early next week, and the maintenance guys were all ready to help out with the hanging. Despite my enthusiasm, I could see a troubled look on her face. She was trying to smile, but it was obvious that something was up. "What's wrong, Marcelee?" I asked. After a pause, she said, "I'd recommend that you avoid 'Larry' for the next several days."

"Larry" (not his real name, for reasons that will soon be obvious) was another library manager and my supervisor at that time. He always seemed to be mostly interested in the library computer system and since my job had little to do with that, he never seemed especially interested in my duties. I did what needed to be done, and he returned positive evaluations and spared me the requirement of frequent and lengthy meetings for the most part. But Larry often seemed very moody, cheerful one day and dark and even cruel in his remarks the next.

One day in the mid-1990's I was walking past Larry's glass walled office and saw a shocking sight on his monitor, which faced the hallway. He was looking at a photo of a nude young man lying on a big rock in a provocative pose. I saw similar images on his computer screen for many months after that when I walked past. For a long time, I convinced myself that he was just looking at pictures, which wasn't all that shocking, since many of our library patrons were looking at pornography regularly on the public internet computers in those days (Marcelee and the library commission had an official policy against the use of software filters on our network to screen out pornographic websites, declaring that it would be censorship to do so).

This continued for years. There was one time that I had a scheduled meeting with him, and when I approached his office, there he was, viewing those pictures. I knocked; he slowly minimized the screen, and then turned around to start our meeting. It was a very uncomfortable situation, obviously. I didn't speak of it, and it was some time before I learned that other staff had seen this behavior too.

He developed an on-the-job interest in South America, with travel books on his desk, South American screen savers, and even a large poster of the pop singer Enrico Iglesias on his office wall, promoting reading. In his later years with the library, he used to go on lengthy vacation trips to South America.

So, when Marcelee told me in that late afternoon meeting to avoid Larry, my first thought was, "like I don't ordinarily?" But instead, I replied, "Why?" She answered, "He's upset with you about your flag idea." I replied, "What's his problem with putting an American flag in a public building?" Her reply was stunning.

"Well, he emails all those *boys* [her emphasis] in South America, and they all hate America's foreign policy, and [Larry] is sympathetic to that point of view."

I replied slowly, "Oh, my God...Oh, my, GOD!" I repeated what she said to be sure I heard her correctly. "He's emailing boys in South America?" This was news to me. She didn't deny it, but just looked away. She had always seemed to be supportive of Larry and his views, and I believe her loyalty toward him was very strong. She looked uncomfortable, perhaps regretting that she had admitted this. But it took a few seconds for me to register what she had just revealed.

I pointed out that several people on her staff had

seen his internet viewing activities, and that it went far beyond just violating city policy. We had children in this library one floor down, and she used to be the children's librarian, for heaven's sake. I was angry, and directed it toward Marcelee. "Why do you allow him to do this?" She shrugged, and said "How am I supposed to stop it? That's just what those kinds of people *do*." Those kinds of people? Was she serious? I replied, "How about saying 'Stop it'?" I shook my head in disbelief. Marcelee seemed to be trapped between two opposing viewpoints from her staff, but made no promises to make Larry cease this extremely inappropriate activity.

I then had to turn this bizarre conversation back to the original subject, my already approved American flag display.

"Marcelee, you've just GOT to go ahead with the flag now. Don't let him talk you out of it." I explained that she had already approved it, and that several people on the staff now knew that it was imminent. There could be no satisfactory explanation for changing her mind. And I told her so. Somewhat surprisingly, she seemed to acknowledge that I was right and agreed with me. She said she would fix this, but she refused to make a firm decision at that moment to allow the flag. "I'll talk to Larry about it tomorrow," she said. I was making a move to leave, and told her once more how imperative it was that she makes him back off and allow us to proceed with the flag as planned. I was sure she would see the logic and do the right thing this time. I wanted so much to believe that. I went home, exhausted and infuriated.

I confided in my father about this exchange that evening. He was angry, saying that he wished I had left that library years ago. "You've got to get out of there," he said. But the money and benefits were good, I had time to ski and travel, I enjoyed my coworkers and felt like they were a second family. Alternative jobs in Boulder were scarce, and I had a very real fear of unemployment after the post-MBA experience. Such tradeoffs allowed me to put up with a lot of aggravations. There were good reasons to stay, if I could just get past this latest crisis. I didn't sleep well that night.

The next day at the library, Friday, was another busy one, and I didn't see Marcelee all day. I didn't get any messages from her, and, as you can imagine, I was not too eager to go upstairs and face Larry. I came in on Saturday, and found this email from her, sent that afternoon from her home:

> From: Marcelee Gralapp
> To: Chris Power
> Date: Sat. Oct 6, 2001 2:12 p.m.
> Subject: flag
>
> I'm going to rescind my offer to put the flag in the coneoid. I've been given nothing but grief from anyone who found out about it and since I was less than hot to do it in the first place, I don't want to proceed any further. However, if the big flag arrives, check to see if it will work on the big flagpole in front of the north bldg.

My immediate thought was, "Larry." He did it. He must have talked her out of it, for purely political reasons. Of course, the flag was too large for the north flagpole, which wasn't tall enough. Besides, if it was objectionable to them to have it in the library entrance, why was it OK to put it on that flagpole? Perhaps because it was so far away that most people would not even guess that the library put it there. Or maybe it was because both she and Larry parked their cars in handicapped spaces every work day right next to the main entrance on the south end of the complex, and neither would have to look at the flag if it was way over on the north side, across the creek and through the woods.

How in the world did Larry have so much influence over her, anyway? I felt sick over this email. Ordinarily, I would get an answer like this, storm upstairs and try, try again to talk Marcelee into doing the right thing. But after the Larry admission, things were different. I would stick to my job duties and not discuss the flag again. I recall thinking that if this decision somehow gets out, I'm just going to "let the chips fall" this time. And did they ever.

.

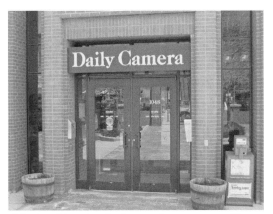

3

The Boulder "*Daily Camera*" newspaper offices

Word Gets Out

The following Monday, I had to let the maintenance guys know that the flag idea had been called off. They were very upset by that decision. Later that day, a woman at the reference desk asked how it was coming along, and I had to tell her that there would be no flag after all. I did admit that Larry talked Marcelee out of it, because that was the truth. That librarian didn't seem at all surprised that Larry would do such a thing.

The library had a powerful grapevine, faster than email, I used to say, and I'm certain that word of this spread to other people. On Tuesday or Wednesday, the Ebay flag from Seattle arrived in the mail. Someone on the staff, who must have known what was in the box, delivered it to my office, jokingly shaking it and wondering aloud, "Is this IT?" A small crowd of library staff gathered as I opened the box and unwrapped the folded flag. The quality was exceptionally good, with thick, bright nylon stripes, and embroidered white stars. One co-worker remarked that it would have looked really beautiful in the coneoid. I was asked what I was now going to do with it, which was a good question. I couldn't return it to the seller, and the city had paid for it, so I was stuck with it. I put it away in my office and tried to forget it.

The next three weeks or so were uneventful, as far as the flag was concerned. While some people on the staff were still talking about it, I began to think that the incident was over, and I would somehow have to pretend that everything was fine, and that I was still part of the team. I followed Marcelee's advice and avoided Larry as much as possible.

I gave some additional thought to that upsetting email reply from Marcelee, the one in which she said that she had been given "nothing but grief from anyone who found out about it," and began to wonder who else, beside Larry, might she have talked to. This third party opposition was a mystery to me, as I had encountered nothing but support from the maintenance and reference staff. So, I asked around. Marcelee's corner office was also all glass, and sounds carried easily. When I asked someone who works within earshot who else she was talking to that Friday about the flag, only two names came up: Larry, of course, and Elizabeth Abbott. I was told that both were vocally against the flag display, and held their ground. Liz was the library's budget analyst in administration who had worked for the city for twenty five years. This same source also quoted Liz as saying at the time, "I think the big flag is a *terrible* idea." So she and Larry reportedly ganged up on Marcelee, and the boss caved. I was not surprised by Larry's opposition to the flag, given his extreme politics, but opposition to an American flag display from Liz was unexpected.

My belief that the flag incident had passed ended abruptly on Friday, October 26. The Tech Logic crew was back in the basement, and I was there working with them when Priscilla, the branch manager, appeared. She took me aside and said that Marcelee was in her office at that moment talking to a reporter "about the flag." Oh, no. I had a sinking feeling from my stomach down to my feet. Nearly three weeks had passed since Marcelee said "no" to the flag, and I thought the secret was safe. "You and your big mouth," Priscilla said. "I didn't call the paper," I insisted, and I hadn't. Besides, plenty of other people knew about the flag, so it could have been anyone. And, I remember telling her that Marcelee was good at handling meddling reporters trying to stir up a new controversy, and that she would find a way to smooth it over. Priscilla seemed to agree with that, and backed off from her accusatory tone.

The next morning, I eagerly tore through the Saturday edition of the Boulder *Daily Camera*, looking for a story about the flag, but didn't find one. I convinced myself that she must have said the right things, and the reporter concluded that there was no story. What a relief. But on Sunday, while reading the paper over my bowl of cereal, it appeared. With an ironic headline, "Flags are Flying in Boulder," reporter Greg Avery opened with, "Flying Old Glory can be a loud political statement in Boulder, where the city's self-image is steeped in its counterculture history." After a brief mention of where flags were on display in Boulder, Marcelee's interview comments appeared, exactly as follows:

Marcelee Gralapp, the Boulder Public Library's art director, recently turned down employee requests to hang a large flag from the glass entrance of the main branch.

"It could compromise our objectivity," Gralapp said, "and we do have many flags outside."

The idea is to make the environment of the library politically neutral to every one of the 2,000 to 3,000 Boulder residents who walk in each day, she said.

"We have people of every faith and culture walking into this building, and we want everybody to feel welcome," Gralapp said.

Library employees can wear flag pins and ribbons, but Gralapp said she urges them to do it thoughtfully.[4]

I dropped my spoon into the cereal bowl. Did she really say that? Our objectivity? I had to think for a moment about the 'many flags' we had outside, before I realized she meant the decades-old flag poles that line the city employee parking lot on Canyon Boulevard. The closest one is almost as far as the length of two football fields from the library's front door, and in the past, they often seemed to lack flags on them, especially in the winter. They would also be used to display the flags of other countries during the World Affairs Conference at the University. I could not recall hearing anything about flag pins and ribbons. And what does it mean to wear a flag pin thoughtfully? I could imagine her, Larry and Liz having a discussion about how the flag would send the wrong political and/or pro-war message, and how inappropriate it would be. And remember, this was before anyone knew of the Bush Administration's plans to in-

4. Greg Avery, "Flags are Flying in Boulder," *Daily Camera*, October 28, 2001.

vade Iraq. But this wasn't a political poster display, or a picture of Uncle Sam pointing and saying "I Want You" to go drop bombs on Afghanistan. It was our *flag*.

I could only console myself that the story appeared in a back section of the paper, and perhaps no one would notice. That was wishful thinking.

At first, I was relieved because there was no reaction in the paper at all for four days. But the following Friday, November 2, 2001, the first two letters to the editor appeared on the subject.

Boulder resident Larkin Hosmer wrote, under the heading, "Boulder Library's Neutrality Foolish," the following letter, which probably attracted as much or more attention than the original article:

> Once again, Boulder has the opportunity to become the laughingstock of the country, only this time, it's not about something as mundane as prairie dogs or pet guardians. Marcelee Gralapp, director at our public library, has determined that flying the American flag is a political statement and hence she will not allow the flag to be displayed in the library entrance.
>
> With the exception of the outermost fringes of our political spectrum, the flag does not represent a political statement. Rather, it shows love, honor and respect for our country—a country that, in case Ms. Gralapp hasn't noticed, is at war because thousands of our citizens and those of other countries were murdered and incinerated by evil people. If Ms. Gralapp is afraid of offending these evil people, too bad. She wants people to feel welcome when they come into the library. Since when has a flag made people feel unwelcome? Hey Marcelee, ever hear of Ellis Island? Do you think we should not have flown the flag there?

I urge our city government to reverse this ridiculous edict and allow the flag to be displayed. If Ms. Gralapp cannot find a flag, I will donate the one that draped my father's coffin. I doubt he thought of the flag as a political statement as he was fighting to keep our country free.[5]

The second letter was written by Paige Rodriguez of nearby Louisville, who could not contain her sarcasm when she wrote, "After all, we know that many of the terrorists have been using our library Internet system to plot their attacks, and we would not want to make them feel uncomfortable by making a bold political statement at the entry of our public libraries." It had been reported that a reference librarian at the Delray Beach Public Library in Florida had seen one of the 9/11 hijack suspects using their computers.

Just past noon that day, an internal email was sent to the entire library staff from Priscilla, under the subject heading, "Publicity." It read,

The library has been the subject of publicity the last few days and there have been many phone calls this morning about the display of the American flag in and around the library. As you know, a number of American flags are flying outside the library on the south [sic] side between us and the municipal building. We have been in touch with the American Legion and flags are in the process of being delivered for display in the meeting rooms for the public at all branches. Staff is certainly welcome and encouraged to share this information with the public.

5. Larkin Hosmer, letter to the editor, *Daily Camera*, November 2, 2001.

So, other than the flags over on the north side, maintained by the city, she acknowledged that there were no flags inside the library, but that there were some on order.

As it happens, I had wrapped up a long week of work with the bookdrop installers, who were on their way back to Minnesota, so I took that Friday off. While driving past the library that morning on my way to the market, I saw a group of protestors with picket signs marching in front of the entrance. The entire base of the stone entryway below the huge dome where I had intended to hang my flag had been covered over with plastic American flags, attached with duct tape. It was a powerful, visual protest. I wondered what kind of turns this story would take from here, and how far it would go, but never imagined the scope of what actually was to come.

On Saturday, November 3, there was a new *Daily Camera* story on the bottom of page one, called "Further flurries in flap over flag." It reported that the group responsible for taping the flags to the building was a half-dozen employees of a high tech Boulder company called Freewave Technologies. They saw the letters to the editor, and went to McGuckin's Hardware store to purchase flags and tape. The firm's chief technology officer, Jonathan Sawyer, said, "This is a government building and this is our country's flag. For them to say this flag could be considered offensive, well, that's just beyond the pale."[6]

For some reason, the reporter must not have been able to reach Marcelee, and spoke to Larry instead. Given my conversation with Marcelee about why Larry did not want that flag put on display, his published comments to the reporter made me angry. He said he "didn't know" that flags had been taped to the building. "The wind will probably blow them away," he said. "I don't think I'll

6. Matt Sebastian, "Further Flurries in Flap Over Flag," *Daily Camera*, November 3, 2001.

probably do anything." The reporter then wrote, "Library employee ['Larry'] pointed out that there are flags at the facility—nine flags outside, between the library and the Boulder Municipal Building, and quite a few inside." Larry told the reporter, "We think it's appropriate to have flags at a government building, and we always have." I cringed at that remark.

The reporter then said that a quick survey inside the library revealed no American flags on display, although a few were seen inside staff offices. One of those offices could have been mine; I had put a small one on my wall.

The location of the frequently mentioned flag poles near Canyon Boulevard, between the north end of the library complex and City Hall, can be seen in the following site plan (note the size of the cars in the parking lots for scale):

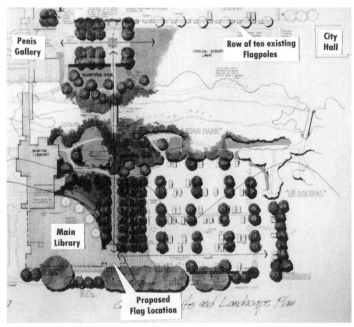

Site plan, by Midyette Seieroe Hartronft Architects,
Boulder, Colorado, 1989

The location of the coneoid, where I proposed hanging the new flag, can be seen at the bottom of this site plan. It is the main entrance to the newest portion of the library, where most of the library functions are concentrated. More than three and a half times as many people use the south doors as those who use the north. As you can see, the row of existing flag poles are separated from the south entrance by two plazas and the heavily forested banks of Boulder Creek.

The Boulder *Daily Camera* wrote an editorial on the subject the following Monday. It said,

> Gralapp's goal as she described it was to make the environment politically neutral to everyone who entered the building. Neutral about what? The democratic values most Americans see in the flag? The warlike values a few individuals read into the flag? The conflict between the United States and terrorism? Whatever she intended to convey, the decision not to display the flag was itself a political statement—a more ambiguous and questionable statement than the flag itself would have made. Displaying the American flag would have implied no endorsement of war and no criticism of any other culture; the flag would have expressed a love for this country and the values for which it stands. Surely the library is not neutral on those subjects. Nor should it be.[7]

Another letter appeared that same day, where Roger Schaefer of Boulder astutely observed, "I get the feeling that it's Ms. Gralapp who feels uncomfortable about being near our flag, not the patrons."

Meanwhile, things were definitely heating up behind

---

7. "Oh, say can you see...What's wrong with flying the flag?" *Daily Camera*, November 5, 2001.

the scenes at the library. I was aware that the city manager's office was going into a crisis mode, and Marcelee was in a lot of meetings over this. Several people on the staff, who knew the score, recognized how difficult this highly visible controversy was on me, and came by my office to express their support. Several made a point to say they supported me in my idea to put up that flag, and were sorry to see me under this kind of pressure.

Someone on the library's maintenance staff told me he got an order from Ron Secrist, city manager, by way of Marcelee, to get an American flag in that main entrance right away. I was told that the maintenance staff searched the library, but could not find a single flag anywhere. They ended up "borrowing" the flag that stood in the city council chambers over in city hall. Obviously, the library had been flag-free. I also recall an episode a few years earlier when an outside group wanting to rent the library auditorium was upset because there was no American flag on the stage, and we didn't have one to lend them.

On Tuesday, November 6, another front page story appeared in the *Daily Camera*, "Stars and Stripes now hang in entry of Boulder library." It said that an American flag on a pole was placed in the entry of the main branch in an effort to reduce criticism of the library. It reported that "On Monday, she (Gralapp) said the decision was based on the size of the flag that employees proposed hanging." Quoting Marcelee, it said, *"People would have had to walk through it to get into the building."*[8]

What? How did she come up with that? She knew exactly how big it was, and that I had carefully measured to come up with the proper size to be seen in that huge glass dome. I was definitely not comfortable with the way

8. Greg Avery, "Stars and Stripes now hang in entry of Boulder library," *Daily Camera*, November 6, 2001.

she was now speaking to the press to get out of this mess she made for herself. In this case, size didn't matter.

The same story quoted city manager Secrist, saying that Gralapp never had any ill intent, nor was she trying to be disrespectful. He said that she made a decision about one location for a flag. Others were on display in other parts of the library, in addition to ones hung daily outside. "It's never been about whether flags will be in public facilities," Secrist said. "She had a specific request about displaying a flag in a way that had never been done before." Why was Secrist saying that? Was he trying to cover up this mess, or was he just going along with what Marcelee had told him? I have no idea. The article said that one of the smaller, donated flags was placed in the entryway on Monday. Perhaps that was the one from the American Legion people, replacing the one from the city council chambers. Then it quoted Marcelee as saying, "Now we have one, and I'm all right with it."[9] That sounded like she was learning to tolerate its presence.

Also that Tuesday, the *Denver Post* printed an editorial that began, "It may come as a shock to Boulder library director Marcelee Gralapp, but, woolly clichés about the 'People's Republic of Boulder' aside, the university town remains a political subdivision of the United States." It said that anybody who might be offended by a flag that represents a country committed to achieving even greater freedoms would be equally offended by the wide selection of books and ideas contained in the library. "In her obeisance to political correctness, it seems to us that Gralapp has performed a contortion heretofore believed to be beyond the physiological limitations of most human beings."[10] Ouch. That was pretty strong for the somewhat liberal *Denver Post*. Perhaps it reflects the an-

9. Ibid.
10. "Long May it Wave," *Denver Post*, November 6, 2001.

ger and anxieties of that post-9/11 time.

A letter to the editor of the *Denver Post* appeared in response to that editorial, from Dick Andrews of Boulder. He wrote:

> Boulder Public Library director Marcelee Gralapp merits induction into the al-Qaeda hall of fame for her refusal to hang this country's flag in the library's entryway. Gralapp seems not to comprehend that we are confronted by an enemy whose avowed goal is to induce a general societal collapse in America, and to kill as many innocent Americans as possible along the way. Osama bin Laden stated recently that Americans lack the social fiber necessary to prevail in the struggle thrust upon us on Sept. 11. For proof of his assertion, bin Laden need look no further than Gralapp's refusal to fly America's symbol. Her comments on the matter display precisely the rot-from-within bin Laden had in mind. Such moral confusion is deeply lamentable in a person holding a public sector leadership position in Boulder.[11]

Another letter to the editor from David Shomper of Boulder said, "I would have hoped that the new flag at the library was hung for more patriotic reasons than 'to reduce criticism of the library'."[12] No, that was the only reason, unfortunately, a bureaucracy trying to save itself from bad press.

Meanwhile, the emails were coming in to the library from all over the nation, via a "comments" link on its web home page, numbering about five thousand, according to press reports. Someone on the staff who had seen them told me that they were very strongly worded, some

11. Dick Andrews, letter to the Editor, *Denver Post*, November 15, 2001.
12. David Shomper, letter to the Editor, *Daily Camera*, November 7, 2001.

48

threatening, and nearly all denouncing Marcelee's stance on the flag. City hall reportedly received about two thousand additional emails. The *Daily Camera* also reported angry email coming to their office from various parts of the country. They said the messages labeled Gralapp "pinko," "un-American," and one recommended that she be shipped out to run a library in Afghanistan.

One of the email messages sent to City Hall was from Esther Coquet of Olympia, Washington, who wrote:

> I am a seventy-five year old widow, but I am an American widow who loves God, family and country above all else. Ms. Gralapp's refusal to allow the American flag to be displayed at the library, stating "it could compromise our objectivity" is an outrage. The freedom to daily use that library was not attained by being "politically neutral," Ms. Gralapp; it was because of the extreme sacrifice of our sons and daughters who fought and died to protect it. Don't make a mockery of their sacrifice.[13]

Councilman Spence Havlick replied, "I think your media source has misreported the facts. We appreciate your concern. Be glad to know flags fly freely in our public buildings and elsewhere in town. And from this we learn that the press may tell only part of a story...perhaps not even the full story and its follow-up."

On Wednesday, November 7, the *Rocky Mountain News* did a story about how an American flag was now unfurled in the lobby of the library, and that "city officials are hoping that the controversy surrounding its appearance will quickly furl and go away."[14] It quoted city

13. Esther Coquet, http://www.ci.boulder.co.us/cmo/citycouncil/hotlist1101.htm Boulder City Council HOTLINE, Number 01-110602, November 6, 2001.
14. James B. Meadow, "Library Waves Old Glory, Ends Flag Flap," *Rocky Mountain News*, November 7, 2001.

manager Secrist, "Ms. Gralapp has served this city for over forty one years and has made tremendous contributions to this community and the library system," and that her position at the library was secure and will not be jeopardized by the flag controversy.

A story also appeared on Denver's evening news, describing the details of the story and saying that Marcelee refused to appear on camera, fearing for her safety. But she told the reporter that she was not making a political statement. "The flag was too big and not appropriate for the location. I didn't feel comfortable having a flag people would have to push aside to get into the building." There it was again.

On Friday, meanwhile, Marcelee sent out the following email to her staff:

> From: Marcelee Gralapp
> To: bpl
> Date: Fri, Nov 9, 2001 4:44 p.m.
> Subject: thanks
>
> To all of you for spending the week dealing with for the most part angry people—on the phone, via e-mail and in person over the flag…issues. I know none of you "signed on" to receive the abuse. And I certainly appreciate that in spite of what your own personal views might be, you have put the library and its principles first. It's not over yet—but I want you to know you have done well and thank you.

The library's principles? Was this some sort of philosophical view about flag displays I missed by not attending library school? I asked two of our professional librarians what Marcelee meant by that, and both said they had no idea. I later asked librarians in other libraries if they would have had a problem putting up a big

American flag after 9/11, and none of them did.

Meanwhile, I was trying to stay out of the controversy, very fearful that some investigative reporter might track me down as the employee who started all this, and start asking questions. If I stuck to the truth, it would contradict what Marcelee and the city manager had already said publicly. I was in a job-saving mode, trying to maintain a low profile.

The Boulder librarian who had banned the American flag became the hottest topic on the talk radio stations in Denver at that time. Since my house was only a seven minute drive to work, I missed out on hearing these radio shows. But I found out that one of the hosts who was particularly outspoken was Peter Boyles of KHOW, a Denver AM station with a regular weekday call-in show, and a television talk show on KBDI Channel 12.

Late in that long week of one news story after another, I came very close to being identified as the unnamed employee "flag guy" on the radio. I came to work as usual, sensing that just maybe the story was losing some steam and dying down. I was determined to get some work related things done that day and not be so stressed. It was time to move on somehow. But when I unlocked my office door, I discovered that the lights were on, and that Steve, our contracted custodian supervisor, was sitting in my chair with his feet up on my desk. He was talking to someone on my telephone.

"What are you doing?" I asked. He waved his hand, as if to say, hold on just a minute. I heard him say to the person on the other end of the line, "You don't know what you're talking about." As I hung up my coat, I continued to listen to his half of the conversation. He said, "You don't *know* the truth. The truth is the flag was just too big for that entrance, and it had nothing to do with politics." I asked, in a loud whisper, "Who IS that?" He again motioned for me to keep quiet. "Well I know what I'm talking about because I'm sitting right next to the guy who bought the flag." I froze. "Who the hell are you talking to?" I demanded. "Get off my phone right now." He again waved me off, saying: "Well, you're wrong, and I can't talk to you anymore." Then he hung up. I demanded, "Who were you talking to?" Steve replied, "That was Peter Boyles. I was on his radio show."

Oh no. He was talking to thousands of Denver area commuters, on my phone. I was mad. What if they called back and got my voicemail? I would be dragged unwillingly into the debate, and would be putting my job in jeopardy. Steve was puzzled as to why I was upset, thinking he was being a good guy by defending the library's position. "You don't know the truth," I told him. "The truth is that it was totally a political decision to ban the flag. I want you to stay out of this, and don't you dare bring my name into it again with anyone."

But the media was just getting started. Something else was about to be revealed that magnified the unwanted attention on the library. The story was about to get even bigger.

4

Hanging 'Em Out to Dry, pixilated. (Photo: Joe Pezillo)

The Dangling Dildos

Marcelee was well known in the local artist's circles as being a big supporter of the arts. She was involved in the formation of the Boulder Arts Commission years ago to provide public funding of art projects. Some of us on the staff believed that after the new library was finished, she appeared to lose most interest in the library and spent most of her time dealing with the politics of the arts interests in town. Her official title was "Library/Arts Director."

When the library was expanded, the traditional public library functions were concentrated in the new building to the south, on Arapahoe Avenue. It was connected to the old building to the north on Canyon Boulevard by an existing indoor "bridge" spanning Boulder Creek. In what used to be the old circulation, fiction and periodicals areas, she specified a 210 seat auditorium, plus an open room that served as an art gallery. Exhibits of all kinds by mostly local artists, some of them quite strange, were put on display in rotation.

On Friday, October 19, just thirteen days after Marcelee had sent me her email that banned the American flag display but only nine days before the flag story appeared in the paper, the library arts staff was setting up an exhibit in the gallery called, "Art Triumphs over Domestic Violence."

I went to lunch that day with Bob Dickie, the marketing director of Tech Logic, our bookdrop maker, at the Walnut Brewery. I had previously informed him of my plans for the flag display right after Marcelee had approved it, but before she changed her mind. Bob seemed genuinely baffled over why she would ban the American flag from her library. He was from Minnesota, trying hard to understand the goings-on of Boulder. We walked back to the library, entering through the Canyon Boulevard doors and into the art gallery, where there was yellow "caution" tape guarding unpacked objects for the new exhibit. Out of the corner of my eye I saw Donna Gartenmann, the staff liaison for the arts commission, on a stepladder, hanging up something on a rope strung near the picture window. I turned around for a second look to see what she was attaching, and with that quick glance, thought, "No, it can't be." Then I stopped talking to Bob, came to a full stop, and turned around once more to face Donna, some twenty feet away. Oh, my God. "Yes Chris, they *are* what you think they are," Donna smiled.

They were, well...penises! They were big and anatomically precise, hanging straight down, of many different colors, and with matching knit cuffs that were used to attach each one to the rope with clothespins. One end of the rope appeared to form a noose. Bob remembers a homeless man on a couch directly under the penises, sound asleep. He says it remains one of his enduring images of Boulder. "What, are you *crazy*?" I asked her. "Does Marcelee know you're doing this?" Donna replied, "Oh, she knows all about it."

On our walk to my office, I told Bob that if the banning of the American flag ever got out, everyone will remark that it's not OK to hang a flag in our library, but it is OK to hang penises. How would they ever be able to explain that?

At the end of that day, as I was heading toward the gallery doors to get to my car, I noticed that the dildos were gone. The rope and clothespins remained. I didn't think much about it at the time. Perhaps they changed their mind, or were going to put them someplace more appropriate. The other exhibits in the show seemed to stay put. The next morning, there was an awards ceremony going on in the adjacent auditorium for the Boulder police department. It would have been a good time for local criminals to do something illegal, because it looked as though every police officer in town was packed into that auditorium.

In mid-morning, I ran upstairs into the office of the arts staff in the north building to make a quick photocopy. There was no one there, and the copier needed to warm up. While waiting, I noticed a large cardboard box at the end of the table with the top opened. I went over and looked inside. There were the dildos, all stacked up. I remember thinking to myself, "Oh good, they came to their senses and are sending these back to where they came from." I reached in and picked up the white one for a closer look. Being a glazed ceramic material, it was quite heavy. The knit cuff on the base end was puzzling. Then I realized that someone might walk in and see me holding this, so I quickly placed it back on top of the boxed pile of penises—"clink." I made my copy and did a hasty exit.

But the dildos reappeared in the gallery that afternoon. Obviously, someone decided to take them down before the police and their guests arrived for the awards ceremony.

Now, let's flash forward nineteen days to the now-public flag flap. On Wednesday, November 7, just one day after the *Daily Camera* reported that a borrowed flag had been placed in the entrance to the library, my fears about the dildo artwork being noticed came true. While I am not sure who broke the story first, I believe that it began on Denver talk radio stations, including the *Lewis and Floorwax Show* and the *Peter Boyles Show*. I didn't hear them myself, but I'm told that they made quite a fuss, as did their callers, and my predicted contrast between the dildos and the flag episode came true.

On Thursday, November 8, the artwork caught the attention of the press. *Fox News* summed it up as, "An American flag might offend people if it's displayed, but apparently ceramic penises won't." It quoted Jonathan Sawyer, who with his staff taped the flags to the library entrance just six days earlier, as saying, "We thought it was just ludicrous, crazy—it's a government building. And then in contrast, to have a controversial exhibit. There's either a total lack of critical thinking or these people harbor some biases that they're trying to impose on others."[15]

The news stories explained that the twenty one ceramic penises were a work called "Hanging 'Em Out to

15. Catherine Donaldson-Evans, "Colorado Library Exhibit Pushes Boundaries of What Defines Art," *Fox News*, November 8, 2001.

Dry" by an artist and student at the University of Colorado named Susanne Walker. It was part of a larger exhibit about domestic violence, sponsored by the Boulder County Safehouse, a women's shelter. The library's cultural program director, Karen Ripley, said, "A lot of this controversy is pure misunderstanding. The flag has been hung all along. The issue is that there was not a flag in one of the entryways." But, as previously stated, I have found no evidence that there were any flags in the entire complex before my suggestion of the entryway display. Then, to defend Marcelee, she said, "She was talking about not flying a 10' × 15' foot flag in the entryway... It would in part cover the entryway in which case people would literally have to lift up the flag to walk in the door."[16]

This was a reiteration of Marcelee's statement to the *Daily Camera* two days earlier, and on Denver television, of her assertion that the flag would somehow be hanging so far down that it would be in people's way. Like the proverbial fish story, that flag just kept getting bigger and bigger. I can't imagine how they came up with this silly notion. Why would I have suggested such a thing? It made no sense.

As for the "Hanging 'Em Out to Dry" display, Ripley told the *Rocky Mountain News* that, from a distance, "they look like socks hanging on a clothesline." Well, perhaps she buys her socks in Amsterdam. She added, "Men find this disturbing, but women find it amusing."[17] The same report quoted the late community activist Ricky Weiser saying that she saw a young boy staring at the clothesline exhibit, and heard his mother say, "No dear, they're corn cobs." But Ripley said the library decided that to deny the display would constitute censorship, and

16. Ibid.
17. Lynn Bartels and Julie Poppen, "Boulder Library's String of Penises' Artwork Miffs Some," *Rocky Mountain News*, November 8, 2001.

decided to let it stay. Of course, putting the dildos behind an enclosed partition, with a warning sign at the opening stating its inappropriateness for children, would have been a sensible option that would have avoided the censorship issue, and perhaps the entire controversy. They didn't do that.

Instead, their open display resulted in some very strong reactions by the public, including this letter from Robert Muchnick, executive director, Center for Children's Justice Inc. in Denver, who wrote:

> The priorities of the savage feminists in Boulder (as in boulders for brains) is nowhere more evident than in the fact the city's library director initially refused to allow an American flag to hang in the library but apparently endorses the display of 21 ceramic penises in the plain sight of children. The message of these enlightened Amazons—including the benighted folks at Safehouse—conveyed with zero subtlety to these children and the rest of civilized society, is that it's OK to castrate the male of the species wholesale. If the Boulder city administration had an ounce of guts they'd call for cultural programs director Karen Ripley's immediate firing, but she'll probably get a cultural achievement award instead because, in her words, 'women find it [the penises] amusing.' I wonder how funny they'd think it was if some divorced fathers who've lost any meaningful contact with their children due to women's vicious perjury and false allegations strung up 21 vulvae in the library.[18]

Another emotional letter to the editor came from Michelle Miller of Erie, who chastised the library officials for not putting such a warning sign before she ar-

18. Robert Muchnick, letter to the editor, *Rocky Mountain News*, November 15, 2001.

rived with her five small children. She wrote, "Despite the vulgarity, and lack of artistic merit, the intent itself is ludicrous. As a survivor of eight years of domestic violence, I can tell you the artist has victimized me again... Domestic violence is not cute, and is rarely about sex (although it may occasionally be employed). More often, it is about having your face smashed into a wall because you didn't do the dishes right." She concluded with, "After viewing the Library's latest contribution to Boulder, my friend and I cut up our library cards and gave them to the director. I urge others to do the same. The Boulder Public Library has become a plank in the eye of the city."[19]

Cindy Crockett, from Centennial, Colorado, provided this exceptionally good perspective:

> As a parent, and former Lakewood High School librarian, I speak to decision-makers in our community. Please consider the children. The decision of those at the Boulder Public Library to not hang our flag was just stupid, but displaying the "string of penises" in a library where parents and teachers take children creates a ripple effect of problems ("Boulder library's 'string of penises' artwork miffs some," Nov. 8). Imagine yourself teaching a newspaper unit with copies of the *Rocky Mountain News* for each student in a middle school classroom on the day when this kind of news is reported. Or taking a group of students to the BPL for a field trip. Or knowing your high school student is going there to do research tonight. Yes, we cherish our freedom from censorship, but with it comes the responsibility to make good decisions. Placing non-controversial material in public and school libraries is not censorship, but wisdom. There is nothing stopping citizens from going elsewhere to get controversial material.

19. Michelle Miller, letter to the editor, *Daily Camera*, November 14, 2001.

Further, as a victim of domestic abuse, I am angered by the concept of hanging male genitalia in a public place. One of the important parts of the healing process for me was to recognize that most men are not abusive. Hanging representations of either sex's genitalia is not a healthy way to ponder men or women. Shame on Safehouse, which is a fine organization in principle, for including this work in its exhibit. I am one woman who does not find this amusing.[20]

Anne Tapp, executive director of Safehouse, told the *Daily Camera*, "What we can hope for is to be impacted by it, to be moved, left wondering and, in some cases, disturbed."[21] Well, it seems that her hopes came true on all four counts.

I also recall seeing this story on the evening news on most of the Denver television channels. My clearest memory is that the photographers didn't quite know how to show the penises on their live, prime time broadcasts. Some photographed only the knit tops attached to the clothesline, while the local *Fox News* channel took shots of it from outdoors, showing them through the window from a distance where they were a bit harder to focus. I was ashamed that everyone in Colorado and beyond was seeing this, and angry as well. None of this should have happened.

It quickly became a national, and international, embarrassment. The Associated Press picked up the story, and it appeared in many major newspapers, including *USA Today*, the *Boston Herald*, and *Newsweek*. The *Columbus Dispatch* in Ohio described the flap, asking

20. Cindy Crockett, letter to the editor, *Rocky Mountain News*, November 15, 2001.
21. Greg Avery, "Body Part Art in Public Library Raises Questions," *Daily Camera*, November 8, 2001.

"What is the deal with Boulder, Colo.?"[22] It was also list-ed as a "Protest of the week" in the *Sunday Times* of London, between a story of a man in Miami attempting to get through customs with forty four songbirds hidden in his pants, and a story of a parrot that learned to keep cats away by barking like a dog.[23] I found an article from something called "*KLIK magazine*" on the web, com-plete with a color photo of the string of dildos, written in Croatian.[24] Other web articles appeared in Hungary and the Netherlands. It was also mentioned in the News-front Forum section of the April, 2002 edition of *Play-boy*, complete with an unusual graphic.

The dildo exhibit inspired outright anger in some people, perhaps best exemplified by comments made by Jann Scott, who hosted a live call-in show on Boulder's cable access channel. Never one to hold back his true feelings, he commented on the display by saying, "The librarian Gralapp should be fired, while the city man-ager hasn't had the balls to even reprimand her and ask, 'what the hell are you doing?'...who the hell is running the show? Shame on them. He should have resigned over this, the librarian should be fired. The people we have running the city completely missed this."[25] Callers to his show were very supportive of his remarks. I can only wonder what his reaction would have been had he known the real story behind the banning of the flag.

There were some humorous moments during the exhibit controversy, and a lot of puns were exchanged among the staff that I'd rather not repeat. One day I passed by the reception desk of the library, near the main

22. "Boulder Caught with its Avant-garde Down," *Columbus Dispatch*, December 1, 2001.
23. This Life, *Sunday Times* (London), Times Newspapers Limited, November 18, 2001.
24. http://www.klik.hr/naslovnica/kultura/200111220002069.html
25. Jann Scott, "Jann Scott Tonight," *Community Access Channel 54*, November 29, 2001.

entrance, and asked the librarian on duty if she had received many questions about the dildo display. She said that lots of people asked about them. While she was talking, I spotted a group of Boulder firefighters in their yellow and green coats and helmets, possibly there after responding to a false alarm. After huddling in the passing crowds for a moment, one large fireman came up to the desk, obviously and awkwardly searching for the right words. The librarian, wanting to spare him the embarrassment, gave him directions to the far north end of the complex to see the now-famous art show. He smiled, relieved that he didn't have to actually ask, and the group of firemen went off in that direction. We had a hearty laugh about that.

My favorite cartoon on the subject was created by Kenny Be in Denver's *Westword*, where he suggests "hanging a string of penis-shaped Old Glories," as shown on the next page.[26]

The three smaller panels refer to other Boulder issues at the time, including road rage, the banning of sofas on porches by the city council to prevent student rioters from setting fire to them, and Boulder's unusually high number of unsolved murders, most famously, that of JonBenét Ramsey.

There were sad moments, too. One that touched me very deeply occurred during the week of the dildo revelations. There were protestors in front of the library at most times of the day, but one stood out. It was an elderly gentleman in a military uniform, the Army I think, holding a small American flag on a short, wooden dowel. He stood alone, about twenty feet from the entrance, making eye contact with people walking from the parking lot. I was watching from upstairs in the business reference room, which has a window that looks out through the big glass dome onto the entrance plaza.

26. Kenny Be, *Westword*, ©2001, reprinted with the permission of Kenny Be and *Westword*, November 22, 2001.

This veteran, smiling at the approaching library patrons, would occasionally cast looks of anger and sadness toward the library, as if he couldn't bear to take one step closer to the place. At that moment, I felt like I was on the wrong side of the window, and wanted to go out there and stand with him. I felt that someone owed this veteran an apology, which he never received.

On the national scene, there was one other story in the news about a library director getting into trouble over banning a patriotic symbol after 9/11, but with a very different outcome.

At the University Library at Florida Gulf Coast University in Fort Myers, the library staff had designed and worn stickers featuring an American flag and the statement, "Proud to be an American." But library director Kathy Hoeth ordered the staff to discontinue wearing them on the job, fearing that they might be offensive to foreign students. When people began to complain, Ms. Hoeth backed off immediately, and issued the following statement that seemed to have put the whole thing to rest. As a contrast to the way the Boulder situation was handled, it bears repeating:

> I would like to express my deepest apologies for the decision I made to ask staff of the University Library to not wear one of the stickers they had designed expressing their patriotism for our country. It was a bad decision on my part, and I have seen and heard first hand today the pain it caused members of the community and the FGCU family of students, faculty and staff. My motivation was to provide a library atmosphere of tolerance and respect for the University's diverse population that represents more than 50 international countries, but the judgment was bad, and I regret the action. I also regret not consulting with the University presi-

dent or provost on my unilateral decision that in no way reflects the views of Florida Gulf Coast University.

I lived in New York for the first 31 years of my life, and like all Americans, I have felt deeply the tragedy that touched not only New York but all of the United States. I am proud of the heroism and bravery that has characterized our country since these tragic events transpired, and I am sorry that my actions appeared contrary to this and caused anguish to anyone.[27]

I admired this librarian so much for changing her mind and making such a sincere and personal apology. But in Boulder, neither Marcelee, nor the city manager ever issued such an apology for the anguish she caused, and she further inflamed the anger with her dildo art show.

In June, 2005, in preparing this story, I put the following question to Carol Brey-Casiano, President of the 64,000-member American Library Association, and director of the El Paso Public Library in Texas: "Do you see anything wrong with displaying an American flag in a public library?" While she emphasized that her views as a librarian were her own and not those of the ALA, she wrote, "I do not see anything wrong with displaying an American flag in a public library. I believe most librarians and library patrons would say that they support the principles that the flag represents. How those principles should be applied in the 21st century might well be a topic for discussion, but a civil, rational debate can only lead to more understanding, so I would consider that a good thing."

When the "Proud to be an American" stickers in the Florida case was mentioned, Ms Brey-Casiano wrote, "I see no harm in wearing them, but those who do should

27. Kathy Hoeth, press release, Office of Community Relations, Florida Gulf Coast University, September 19, 2001.

realize that they can be inflammatory and should be prepared to have a serious conversation about why they put them on. Still, if you require someone to take off a pin [or sticker] only because its message might offend others, you are trampling on one of the principles we support most ardently: the First Amendment, which guarantees freedom of speech."

Well said. These statements confirmed my suspicions that Marcelee's principles did not fall within the mainstream of the public library community. I chose not to ask the ALA president for her position on hanging dildos in public libraries.

The passionate debates and widespread publicity led to the next weird part of this story, when an angry citizen decided to take the matter of the dildos into his own hands, so to speak.

5

Bob Rowan under the clothesline, describing to the
media the ones that got away. (Photo: Joe Pezillo)

The Dildo Bandito

At the end of that long week, I came to work at the library on Saturday morning, November 10, relieved that everyone else in Administration would be gone and things might be a little more peaceful. My wishful thinking proved wrong again.

I came in through the Canyon Boulevard entrance, and as I entered the art gallery, I saw two Boulder police officers, one of them interviewing a woman who appeared to be very upset. Next to them was the now-famous clothesline, but...the penises were gone. I had seen this before, but this time, there were no police awards ceremonies scheduled that day.

The clothespins remained, but there was something else clipped to the center of the rope. It was a sheet of paper, with a small American flag taped to it. I moved closer to read what was written on the paper. In hand-scrawled printing, it said, "El Dildo Bandito was here—God Bless America." My first reaction was to laugh out loud for a second or two, before I noticed the two policemen looking up at me, suspiciously. Backing off, and holding my hands up in the air, I declared, "Oh, I *work* here!" Just when I thought this story couldn't get any weirder, it did.

One of the young officers was taking notes as the upset woman, who may have been the artist, spoke. He had a funny expression on his face, like he really didn't sign on to be a cop to deal with, well, this kind of theft. My impression is that the other officer was trying hard not to grin over the situation. But they had my sympathies, as the unsolved JonBenét Ramsey murder case was still very much on people's minds, and this was the last thing the Boulder police needed to deal with, stolen dildos.

Unlike that murder case, the police got a break right away on a suspect. A man named Bob Rowan phoned a Denver radio station, bragging that he had taken the penises out of the library and wanted to talk about it on the air. The station's producer got his name and address and then called the Boulder police.

I arranged a meeting with Mr. Rowan over two years later, to exchange our stories. The police had just returned his flag, found after they cleared out a storage locker. It was confiscated at the time as evidence. He provided me with some details that were not published at the time.

The then-forty nine year old contractor is a resident of the Heatherwood neighborhood in northeast Boulder. He told the *Denver Post* that he understands the point of the exhibit and supports the work of the shelter in helping battered women. But he was angered that the library didn't consider the feelings of families and their children. Rowan said, "They fall real short of having any respect for our community. If they had put this up at a private art gallery, that would have been fine. That way people could pay and see this stuff."[28]

He told me that his wife woke him up at about 1:30 a.m. Sunday morning, saying that there was someone at the door. He was stumbling as he went to the door, having had some drinks that night after a day of pilfering penises. He opened the door and said there were "three Boulder cops" standing there. They asked if he had stolen the artwork from the library, and he confessed, saying that he intended only to get them out of view of the children and planned to return them to the artist right away. The police asked him to produce the stolen dildos, and he replied that they were still in his truck.

He ambled over to the truck in the dark with the police following closely behind, and unlocked the door. He told me that he had recently been on a hunting trip. When the door was opened and the police aimed their flashlights inside, they saw a dozen or so spent shell casings on the floor. According to Mr. Rowan, all three police officers immediately drew their guns and pointed them at him, as if to say, "Your dildos or your life!" Wouldn't one gun have been sufficient? Mr. Rowan immediately put his hands in the air, and told them the artwork was in the cardboard box in the back. The police retrieved the box, but it was dildo-free. Then his wife came from the house with a white plastic bag, filled with them. He was not arrested because the artist had not yet decided to press charges.

He told the *Rocky Mountain News*, "My intent was not to break and smash them. I told police, here's the box,

28. Monte Whaley, "Art Thief: Library lacked respect," *Denver Post*, November 12, 2001.

69

I was going to mail them back. I wanted them down; I didn't want the stupid things."[29]

Mr. Rowan—who's daughter, Alison, was five years old at the time—questioned the educational benefit of such an exhibit, saying, "I can't imagine any teacher of any school taking a classroom of kids to see this."

After artist Susanne Walker reportedly decided not to press charges and refused to rehang the reclaimed penises in the library, prosecutors declined to press criminal charges since Mr. Rowan did not intend to keep the stolen dildos. This decision to not rehang prompted a "hotline" email from City Councilman Spense Havlick, who wrote, "It is very troubling to think that protests and threats from far away could influence our staff about showing an important social message in an art form. Will there next be a protest that Mao's Red Book or a photo essay showing nude Roman or Greek gods or goddesses be banned from the library shelves?"[30]

When Bob Rowan and his wife Kathryn arrived at the police station on Tuesday, they were wearing custom T-shirts bearing his nickname "El Dildo Bandido" and the American and Mexican flags.

Speaking of the display, he told a reporter, "It's a real kick in the groin to our boys," referring to the military forces preparing for battle in Afghanistan. "Pornography does not belong in our library. Maybe we need private libraries, and the mayor and librarian can enjoy their own."[31]

Of course, many people in Boulder were horrified by what Rowan had done. Boulder resident Louise Padden was not offended by the artwork, but she was by

29. Owen S. Good, "Phallus Art puts Father in a Fury," *Rocky Mountain News*, November 12, 2001.

30. Spense Havlick, Boulder City Council hotline, number 01-111402, November 14, 2001.

31. Christine Reid, "Bandito charged in library exhibit's theft," *Daily Camera*, November 14, 2001.

Rowan's actions. "I think, as a father, he would under-stand one of the things he wants his child to understand is impulse control. There are more mature ways of han-dling situations we don't agree with."[32]

A day or two after his run-in with the authorities, I was in my office at the library when I got a frantic call from one of the staff at the switchboard, located near the now famous art gallery. She said there was some kind of disturbance forming outside, and she was alone down there—what should she do? I sensed some genuine ter-ror in her voice. I said I would be right there, and bolted down the hallway. When I got to the gallery, I looked through the windows and saw a group of around fifteen people in white T-shirts, carrying American flags. I lat-er learned that one of the people in the crowd was Mr. Rowan himself. He was carrying a very large American flag on a long pole. As the group moved toward the door, I was ready to dial 911, expecting some sort of a riot.

But they got the idea to move over to the edge of Canyon Boulevard instead, a major thoroughfare in town. Mr. Rowan waved the giant flag in view of the passing cars as the group held up signs. I went into the enclosed courtyard garden next to them, unseen, for a look. Near-ly every single passing car honked their horns wildly in support. It again demonstrated to me how out of touch our "public" library was with the people we were sup-posed to serve. The group moved back toward the plaza in front of the gallery doors, but never attempted to come inside. I felt a responsibility to protect my beloved library, but also secretly wanted to get into one of their T-shirts and join in. I hated being in that position.

During that second week of debate and attention, Bob Rowan was awaiting his fate. While the police said they were not inclined to press theft charges since Rowan

32. Ibid.

intended to return them to the artist, many in Boulder wanted him arrested. And the local chapter of the ACLU got involved, with Chairman Barry Satlow sending a letter to the police, the DA, and the local papers, demanding Rowan's arrest, to protect the artist's First Amendment rights.

He wrote, "We understand that, although Mr. Rowan admitted the theft to the Boulder police, the police department has decided not to charge him unless the artist requests it. Ironically, this is the way domestic violence has historically been treated, with police declining to arrest or charge unless the victim chose to press charges."[33]

Jane Gamble of Morrison, Colorado wrote a unique idea in a letter to the editor: "Robert Rowan, the Dildo Bandito, could have avoided being charged by Boulder police in the Case of the Purloined Penises. If he had claimed to be a 'performance artist,' then removing Susanne Walker's installation would be interpreted as 'self-expression,' and the ACLU could defend Rowan on the grounds that his First Amendment rights were being violated."[34]

After rejecting a plea deal, Bob Rowan appeared before Boulder County Court Judge Thomas Reed (his wife just happens to work for the Boulder Public Library). Rowan pleaded guilty to a misdemeanor charge and was assessed a small fine. He told the *Camera*, "In my wildest imagination, I never figured this would get so much frickin' attention."[35]

During a panel discussion on Denver public television, legal analyst and local radio personality Craig Silverman questioned Bob Rowan's real motives. "I have to think that a guy like Bob Rowan is really in it for his personal attention. If he was really concerned about the

33. Ibid.
34. Jane Gamble, letter to the editor, *Denver Post*, November 17, 2001.
35. Greg Avery, "'Bandito' awaits artist's decision," *Daily Camera*, November 13, 2001.

sensitivities of his young daughter, would he take on the name, 'El Dildo Bandito?' What's the five year old going to say, 'My father is El Dildo Bandito?' It doesn't have a lot of class." Panelist David Kopel of the Independence Institute added, "Stealing the art was wrong, but I have to say that the Boulder librarian has made their library an international laughing stock."[36]

As a result of his notoriety, Mr. Rowan was encouraged to enter local politics. He announced before his court hearing that he was considering a run for Representative for State House District 10, which includes Gunbarrel, Niwot and portions of Boulder. He was concerned that a criminal record because of the penis theft could jeopardize his political ambitions. Mr. Rowan told me that the time required to run for office conflicted with his need to continue his contracting business, and passed on the idea.

Rowan was the main topic of conversation on Denver talk radio for days. The vast majority of callers thought he was an American hero. The Boulder police chief, Mark Beckner, told the *Rocky Mountain News* they had received calls from both sides of the issue. "Some people think we should throw this guy in jail and other people think he should be given an award." The artist, Susanne Walker, placed a statement at the library display, calling the theft "an attack on my freedom of speech." She wrote, "It makes a joke of the pain and suffering involved in this exhibit." She demanded that the thief confront her in person, saying, "If you want to attack me or my artwork, then confront me with discussion."

Not one to back off, Rowan declared, "There is no face to face discussion. I'd be glad to stare at her, but we won't have a conversation on what the value of her art

---

36. Craig Silverman and David Kopel, "Colorado Inside Out," KBDI Public Television, November 23, 2001, used with permission.

is. Not in our public library, anyway. You don't hang penises and then discuss what the value is." He added, "I'm just so ticked about the whole deal, I can't believe it."[37]

When I met Mr. Rowan in that meeting more than two years later, he showed me part of his large collection of letters of support from across the nation. He also mentioned to me that the city hired him several months after that whole ordeal to do some plaster work on an outside wall of, believe it or not, the main library. I doubt the city realized his not-so-secret other identity, and to Mr. Rowan, it was "just another job."

I should also mention a very strange coincidence. While searching for books about patriotism on Amazon. com in 2004, I came across a photography book about how people responded to the events of 9/11, with every picture featuring an American flag on display in some way. It was called "Old Glory and Friends." What caught my eye was the name of the author and photographer: Bob Rowan! But it was a different one, from Newport, Washington, not *our* Bob Rowan. The "Bandito" was greatly amused to see his name on that book, and obtained a copy for himself.

What can I say about the "Bandito?" Just for the record, I also believe that stealing art is wrong, of course. But I think that his heart was in the right place. He knew that neither the library nor the artist would ever remove the dildos on their own, no matter how many people complained, so he made a drastic move. I admire him for tackling what was a mostly impenetrable bureaucracy that needed to be shaken up, and for speaking out about his beliefs. And he certainly provided some much needed humor to this strange story.

Now, in the interest of equal time, let's hear from the artist.

37. Owen Good, "Phallus Art puts Father in a Fury," *Rocky Mountain News*, November 12, 2001.

Opening Reception at the Art Show (Photo: Anon.)

Artist Susanne Walker Responds

Since I was able to find and meet Bob Rowan, I also wanted to meet Susanne Walker to get her side of this story. But her Boulder phone had been disconnected, and no one knew where she had moved. After months of trying, I received an email from her on June 13, 2005 after she received a forwarded letter that I had sent to an old address. She resisted a telephone interview, but agreed to answer a set of written questions.

She added the following statement to her reply: "Please keep in mind the penalties associated with libel. If you plan on using any of this information, it has to be directly quoted unless I grant permission for change. I do not wish to have any of my statements taken out-of-context or paraphrased." Fair enough. So here are my questions and Susanne's answers exactly as they were received.

> **Power:** *How did you become involved in the "Art Triumphs Over Domestic Violence" exhibit at the library?*

> **Walker:** There were published announcements and a call for entry. I simply applied to be in the show like all the other artists involved.

> *What was the idea behind the "Hanging 'Em Out to Dry" exhibit, or what message were you trying to convey?*

> It was a statement about the set-up of our patriarchal society in which everyday women are exploited. When broken down into body parts, in this case genitalia, it is more excepted and common to see women; men are rarely portrayed in this manner.

> *The title seems somewhat violent, suggesting castration and/or vengeance—was that the intent?*

> This question implies the diminished level of comfort one may have when viewing penises rather than other body parts. The art is in no way suggesting or intended to suggest violence, vengeance, or castration.

> *Was there a meaning to the knit cuffs, or were they just a practical way to attach to the rope with clothespins?*

> I hand-knit the cuffs for the penises in order to comically represent pairs of socks that you would see hanging on a clothesline. This was analogous to an accepted image we see in society...socks hanging on a line. Also for clarification, the one white penis was intended to be the one white sock you al-

ways lose in the laundry, not some white supremacy statement like the media portrayed. In addition, the clothesline was NOT tied in a noose, nor intended to be displayed/look this way.

Was there any discussion with you and the library staff about where to hang them? Was there ever a location mentioned besides the picture window?

Artists were not involved in the display and I did not know where my piece would be hanging until I came to the opening reception. Your question implies that they were directly in the middle of the window, this is untrue. In actuality, the work was strung between two pillars diagonally away from the window. *[Note: As a clarification, based on photographs I obtained, she is correct that the clothesline was strung between two interior pillars by someone on the staff, but only for that opening reception. Before and after that evening, the rope was stretched between a hook on the wall a few inches from the window, and a structural column about two feet in from the window, as shown in the Chapter 5 photo. It appeared that someone coiled and knotted the rope where it was hooked to the wall to take up slack, causing it to look somewhat like a noose, hence the confusion.]*

Can you at least understand why some people who knew nothing about you or the theme of the show found the exhibit so inappropriate for a public library, or even offensive? What would you say to them?

This question implies that I don't understand the implication of my own artwork. People form opinions about everything; I cannot control whether someone becomes offended. I would say that I have a constitutional right to the freedom of expression without being censored in such a blatant way. The intention of art in any form is to inspire and fuel discussion…"Why does this bother you? Let's look into that…" Art has been doing this for thousands of years and some of the most controversial pieces obviously are powerful enough to elicit this reaction. I do not think that my display was inappropriate for a gallery that happens to be in the library. There were signs up about the exhibit and what the exhibit was for. Let us also remember the context of the art show, for which my work was displayed. The whole idea behind the show was to give voice to survivors of domestic violence and/or sexual assault. I believe my work was completely within context of all the other pieces there. Anytime a show is done about violence, it is probably going to be emotional, challenging, and make some people angry.

Do you believe Mr. Rowan should have had a greater punishment than a one month deferred sentence?

I think that we have laws in place for when someone commits a crime. Mr. Rowan committed a punishable crime and he should have been prosecuted to the fullest extent of the law. It should not have been left to me to decide whether to press charges, it just should have been done. Ironically this mirrors how so many survivors of domestic violence experience the system and it is unfortunate. The problems with Mr. Rowan's actions are that just because you don't like or agree with something, doesn't mean you can go in, steal and damage it. There are lawful and peaceful ways to protest.

I know that the art was returned to you and you decided not to rehang them in the library. What happened to them since then? Were they ever displayed elsewhere? Sold?

I did not decide to not re-hang the work. Safehouse, the library, and the city made the decision. I agreed to this because I did not want to see any other artwork compromised or any other artists, let's remember, many of whom were survivors, to be further traumatized by a society that already sees them only as victims. One pair was sold for charity at an auction in Boulder, five individual penises were just recently returned to me by the Boulder Police property and evidence department (the ones damaged/broken by Mr. Rowan), and the others are now in my collection of work. One dark blue penis was never returned upon original recovery by the Boulder Police.

Can I mention what you are doing now, or do you want to keep that quiet?

I am at the University of Michigan pursuing graduate study in Social Work. I will graduate with my MSW in December of this year. I am also a volunteer sexual assault counselor/advocate and work as a research assistant at the University.

I would like to add that this exhibit was up for almost a month and not a single person that went to the show had complained or displayed public offense. It was not until the statement was made on Peter Boyles' radio show protesting the library not hanging the giant flag that any attention even came to my artwork. Both media and private citizens, coming home from work to an average of thirty messages on my answering machine, harassed me for many months. In reality, this show had ABSOLUTELY NOTHING to do with a flag; it had to do with the pain, suffering, and survival of survivors of interpersonal violence. My hope is that you will keep this in perspective as you write your book since the reality of the art show/event has rarely been mentioned.

[I asked her this follow-up question by email:]

I understand your statement about how art should fuel discussion, without censorship. But there was a lot of criticism that the art was clearly visible to children coming through that door. You didn't mention the issue of children in your reply. How would you respond to those critics who believed the artwork was inappropriate for children passing by?

The question regarding my response to children is a good one. Considering that the gallery has a completely separate entrance and even parking lot than the main library, parents should be able to control, with adequate warnings, signs, etc. what going through that entrance would entail. Even coming from the main entrance of the library and crossing over into the gallery, the type of art show was well advertised. Please remember that my piece was not the only piece that showed body parts and the whole theme of the show circulated around domestic violence. It is ultimately the responsibility of the child's guardian to clarify and answer the child's questions, not my responsibility as an artist to censor my work for a show that clearly is about survival through violence. Again, my piece was well within context. Children are exposed to all types of visual stimuli everyday of their lives. Interestingly enough, children that did go to the show and I received reports back from parents, understood the sock idea, an analogy that adults and the media over-looked. Adults like to read into thing and over-analyze too much. They take something and mold and shape it into the context they want it to portray.

7

Politicians Jump Into the Flag Flap

Susanne Walker's answers were very insightful. I appreciated her response and wish her well. But one sentence in her answers raises another curious question. Just what, do you suppose, ever happened to that missing "dark blue penis" that was in the custody of the Boulder Police Department? We may never know.

Now, let's get back to the post-dildo media circus. The Boulder *Daily Camera* reported that on Thursday, November 8, 2001, the same day the news of the "dangling dildo" artwork began to appear, that Colorado's own U.S. Senator, Ben Nighthorse Campbell got into the fray by sending a letter to Boulder Mayor Will Toor. The Senator wrote:

Accompanying this letter is a cloth flag which has flown over our nation's Capitol. I send it to you and the city of Boulder as a gesture of good will but also to emphasize what this symbol stands for at a time when our nation is defending the freedoms we hold dear. This weekend we celebrate Veteran's Day to honor the men and women of all races and religions, including some who made the ultimate sacrifice to preserve the freedom of people like Boulder Public Library director Marcelee Gralapp to offend so many in the name of free speech.[38]

Mayor Toor replied to the Senator, declining the offer and telling him that one flag was already on display when an employee requested another, and that there are twelve flags in and around the library. No, Mr. Mayor, I actually suggested the flag on October 3, and the first flag didn't appear in the library until November 5. There were absolutely no flags in the library before that, or outside by the main entrance, and the row of ten flags over on Canyon Boulevard was very distant from my proposed location.

Easing up on its earlier, scolding tone, a *Daily Camera* editorial said, "The library hullabaloo has been awash in emotion and bereft of reason. Gralapp offered an odd justification for not flying a particular flag in a particular place. But that does not make her a traitor, and it doesn't link her to the Taliban. It should not subject her to nationwide ridicule."[39]

Indeed, in the midst of all the criticism of Marcelee, there were some opposing views of support. Alma Becker of Boulder wrote to the editor, "Could we please cut

38. Senator Ben Nighthorse Campbell, "Campbell: Flag Stands for Freedom & Diversity," press release, http://www.senate.gov, November 8, 2001.

39. "Venom of Intolerance, Library debate goes from bad to worse," *Daily Camera*, November 14, 2001.

Marcelee Gralapp some slack on this flag thing? The flag is a symbol, and the symbol changes with the times and the context. Right now, slapping a flag on the glass entrance of the library says more than that we are Americans... Immediately after Sept. 11, the flag suggested American pain, grieving, shock."

She continued, "This has evolved so that the current context to displaying the flag is to be a supporter of the war and the bombing of Afghanistan. Not every library patron believes that we should be doing so, and thus it would be a clearly politicized statement."[40]

Ms. Becker actually makes an interesting point, although I don't believe for a minute that displaying our flag at that time was an automatic endorsement of going to war. But I think if Marcelee had said something like this in that original interview instead of speaking of her fear of compromising objectivity, being unwelcoming and remaining politically neutral, she just might have gotten away with it.

Not all of Boulder's self-proclaimed liberals were in agreement on this flag issue. Jessica Sandler of Boulder wrote, "How does one get appointed arbiter of what the U.S. flag represents?" She cited the above mentioned letter from Ms Becker. "As I fly my flag to express my solidarity with New York and my country, I am ashamed of many of my fellow liberals—for their feeble attempts to rationalize the assault, for rushing to criticize America, and for their hypocrisy in supporting corrupt, autocratic Arab regimes while viscously attacking Israel..." She also criticized conservative writers, and ended with, "whatever camp that puts me in, my American flag still flies."[41]

Marcelee's position was vigorously defended by a writer who goes by the name "Dark Cloud," in an arti-

---

40. Alma Becker, letter to the editor, *Daily Camera*, November 10, 2001.
41. Jessica Sandler, letter to the editor, *Daily Camera*, November 10, 2001.

cle on his website. This person apparently believed much of the misinformation put out by Marcelee and the city, writing:

> Although the walkways between city hall and the library's main branch have been festooned with Old Glory and even though several flags are included in the library's interior decoration, heroic employees of the library announced that they wished to hang a giant, ten by fifteen foot flag in the entrance area. Never mind that flag etiquette requires a flag to be hung from a pole, or that such a giant hankie would wipe the faces of people in and out, or that it was a really childish idea. Marcelee Gralapp, the Library's director, forbade it. She said a library was open to all and perhaps felt it was not the place for such ostentatious display of war lust, which the additional huge flag would have been. I agree and have been nauseated by the pandering to morons by city government, city newspaper, and the local wowsers. What was obvious about all this was that it was a setup to attack Gralapp conceived by library employees and orchestrated by her bureaucratic and civilian enemies who resent the forty year employee of Boulder and the city's living symbol of bureaucratic, liberal power.[42]

Oh my. Well, I will just say that in no way was my flag suggestion a setup of Marcelee.

An editorial in a South Carolina newspaper added to the discussion, focusing on the appropriateness of such an exhibit in a tax supported building:

> One might say we only have to avoid art, or anything else, which offends us. And this is true, as

---

42. Dark Cloud, "Pseudo Patriots, Boulder's Head Librarian Faces Down the Mob," www.darkendeavors.com, November 7, 2001.

true as the fact we can change the channels on our televisions and not shell out the money for yet another double-entendre saturated cinema non-classic that passes for a movie. But it's pretty hard to avoid a clothesline of body parts in a public building. One can't exactly change the channel or decide not to spend the money on something they consider in poor taste. It's already spent, every time the tax bill comes. Don't be surprised to hear that in Boulder, they've shelved this library director and gotten a new one. If so, it's likely almost no one will be offended.[43]

And Patricia Calhoun, editor of a popular Denver weekly newspaper, wrote, "By its very nature, a library is the sort of place where tough topics, including domestic violence, deserve to be discussed. But such discussion belongs in books, and arguably in sections that can be closed off to those who'd rather read about the subject than see it when they enter the public facility—or, more to the point, have their children see as they enter."[44]

There was a lot of material on the internet about the Bandito, including some lively discussions debating if Rowan was a hero or a criminal. The puns were rampant, with this laugh-out-loud favorite from an anonymous contributor: "Urethra for him or against him."

In another relatively minor story, a second piece of art from that same Safehouse exhibit was stolen, this time a nude torso. But it was later recovered in a downtown dumpster. The entire domestic violence exhibit was removed a short time later.

Another politician in Washington got involved in

43. "Symbolism Gets No Sympathy," *Anderson (S.C.) Independent-Mail*, November 29, 2001.
44. Patricia Calhoun, "How's it Hanging? Life in the Penis Gallery and Other Mixed Nuts in Boulder," *Westword*, ©2001, reprinted with the permission of *Westword*, November 15, 2001.

the debate, U.S. Representative Tom Tancredo, a Republican from Golden, Colorado. During that second week, shortly after the Dildo Bandito had struck, I was at home, anticipating an evening of distraction from all this by watching television. As I was scanning the channels, I landed on CSPAN2, and saw Tancredo speaking before Congress. He was denouncing the banning of patriotic symbols around the country, mentioning the banning of draped flags on fire engines in Berkeley (which officials there said was done for fear they might provoke anti-war demonstrations). But then he mentioned the banning of the flag in the Boulder Public Library. He spoke about it in a very passionate, exasperated tone.

My brother happened to be there at the time, and I summoned him to the TV quickly. He watched in equal astonishment this national airing of our flag flap. Looking at me, my brother said, "I can't believe you started this." Neither could I.

Tancredo then introduced his "Freedom to be a Patriot Act" on October 31, 2001. It called for a denial of any Federal funds to institutions that chose to ban patriotic symbols. In Congress, he spoke of universities that were reportedly told to remove patriotic displays because they might offend international students. But he described the Boulder flag and dildo controversy because it struck closer to home and got him thinking about the issue. Tancredo told the *Denver Post*, "It was like this incredible gift I was given to explain this issue, that people would be offended by the flag, but not by this."[45] This, of course, being the penises.

Once again, the City of Boulder failed to tell the truth. The *Colorado Daily* reported that city spokesperson Jana Peterson told them that, "...the library has

45. Mike Soraghan, "Tancredo Bill takes Offensive on Flag," *Denver Post*, November 20, 2001.

no federal funds to take. In 2000 the library received no funds from the federal government."[46] I don't know where she got her information, because as Marcelee knew, I procured federal funding from the "E-rate" program for schools and libraries each year to help pay for our internet and phone services. Being public information, if you go to their website and look it up, you will see that the Boulder Public Library was granted $13,692.74 in 1999, $17,468.64 in 2000 and another $13,884.15 in 2001.[47] The actual amount of federal funds received by the library in 2000 was $16,510.92.

As for Berkeley, Mayor Shirley Dean had ordered the flags put back on the fire engines, which to her showed that Tancredo's bill wasn't needed. "I really think localities can be trusted to handle these matters ourselves." Tancredo admitted that the bill had little chance of passing and was a warning shot to bureaucrats not to put political correctness ahead of patriotism. In fact, there were several editorials and letters to editors that didn't care for the idea of this bill, and it ultimately did not pass. But the fact that my suggestion of hanging a flag in our library resulted in a debate on the floor of Congress less than two months later was just astounding to me.

The flag/dildo flap did not fade away quickly. In fact, it made national news again more than a year later, in 2003. Joe Scarborough, host of "MSNBC Reports," a cable news show, talked about legislation proposed in the Colorado State Senate to protect the right to fly the flag. The introductory trailer stated, "Flying the American flag whenever and wherever you want...sounds like a given, right? Not in Boulder, Colorado."[48]

46. Michael A. de Yoanna, "Congressman irked over library flap," *Colorado Daily*, November 21, 2001.

47. http://www.sl.universalservice.org E-Rate Funding Commitments, 1999-2001.

48. Joe Scarborough, *MSNBC Reports*, MSNBC, March 3, 2003.

State Senator Doug Lamborn, a Republican from Colorado Springs (a city with a reputation for being as conservative as Boulder is liberal) appeared on the program. His proposed bill stated, "A person shall have the right to display reasonably the flag of the United States or other commonly recognized emblems or symbols of the nation or of a person's patriotism, on one's person, property, in schools, or in any tax-supported property in the state."[49] Mr. Scarborough asked the Senator, "Why in the world do you feel it was necessary to legislate this kind of protection? Isn't it protected by the United States Constitution?" Lamborn replied, "Well they are, but you heard about that outrageous incident in Boulder."[50] His bill passed, but with amendments giving local governments the ability to adopt rules concerning the size, number, placement and lighting of flags. It is not clear if Marcelee could have been prosecuted for her flag ban, had this law been in effect at the time.

I would like to wrap up the public debates and outcry by reprinting two very different but excellent viewpoints. The first was written by Paul Danish, a former county commissioner and city council member, best known for being one of the founders of the movement years ago to impose strict limits on growth in Boulder. He tries to analyze what was really going on with Marcelee's thinking. He wrote:

What's Hangin' at the Library?
By Paul Danish

Shortly after the jets hit the World Trade Center and the Pentagon, several employees of the Boulder Pub-

---

49. Senators Lamborn, Andrews, Arnold, et al, Colorado Senate Bill 03-235, "AN ACT, Concerning the Right to Display the United States Flag," approved May 14, 2003.
50. Senator Doug Lamborn, interview by Joe Scarborough, *MSNBC Reports*, MSNBC, March 3, 2003.

lic Library asked the head librarian for permission to fly a 10-by-15-foot American flag on the building's south side facing Arapahoe. Permission was refused—a fact that didn't go unnoticed by right-wing talk radio hosts (are there any other kind?).

Some 2,000 e-mail messages to city hall later (most of them nasty-grams), three explanations emerged. I don't buy any of them.

1. The explanation that the library chose not to fly the flag in order not to offend someone is both dishonest and silly. Dishonest because at the same time it was refusing to show the flag it was hosting an antidomestic violence art exhibit that included Hanging Them Out to Dry, which featured a string of ceramic penises. Obviously the artist was trying to shock and offend in order to make her point. Just as obviously the library understood and affirmed the strategy. So what's wrong with offending Osama bin Laden?

2. The suggestion that the library chose not to fly the flag because dozens of flags are already flying in front of it misses the point. An extraordinarily evil event cries out for an extraordinary response. That's why thousands of public and private buildings that routinely fly the flag put up bigger and more prominent ones after 9/11.

3. The explanation that the library didn't want to fly the flag because it was afraid it would compromise its objectivity is the most substantive alibi, but it doesn't wash either. Yes, a library should function as the honest broker in the marketplace of ideas, but it is also incumbent on it to be a fierce partisan for at least one set of ideas—freedom of thought, speech and belief and tolerance for the thought, speech and beliefs of others. That idea lies at the

core of America's quarrel with bin Laden. And a library has no business being neutral in this particular struggle—anymore than the library at Alexandria should have been neutral in the war with Theodorus.

So what's the real reason that Marcelee Gralapp, Boulder's chief librarian and one of the town's great good hearts, chose not to fly the flag?

I suspect it's because librarians, like generals, sometimes prepare to fight the last war, and that Marcelee was viewing the issue through the lens of Vietnam, when the symbols of patriotism were used as weapons in the domestic debate over the war.

Bad choice. This war is different.[51]

The next viewpoint was a column written by Mike Rosen, a conservative writer and radio personality in Denver. His column from the *Rocky Mountain News*, while obviously over the top in many ways, was one of my favorites.

Library Escapade Reveals PC Fallacy
By Mike Rosen

WARNING: THIS COLUMN MAY BE OFFENSIVE TO READERS WHO ARE UNCOMFORTABLE WITH REFERENCES TO SEXUAL ORGANS, AMERICAN FLAGS OR BOTH.

The People's Republic of Boulder, the city of alternative lifestyles, flower children, aging hippies, granola heads, earth mothers, ivory tower intellectuals, kinder and gentler cops and prosecutors, and unisex ponytails has managed to embarrass itself

---

51. Paul Danish, "What's Hangin' at the Library?" *Coloradan, the University of Colorado Alumni Magazine,* February, 2002, reprinted with permission of the author and the *Coloradan.*

yet again and tick off just about everybody in the process.

You've no doubt heard by now. But just to review, it all started when Marcelee Gralapp, the director of the Boulder Public Library, rejected the request of employees to drape a 10-by-15-foot American flag from the building's entrance as a heartfelt display of patriotism and love of country in the wake of the Sept. 11 terrorist attack. Gralapp's explanation at the time, as told to the Boulder *Daily Camera*, was that "it could compromise our objectivity." "We have people of every faith and culture walking into this building, and we want everybody to feel welcome," she added.

Clearly stated. But I disagree with her appraisal of the situation and her judgment, as did a letter writer to the *Camera* who wondered why an American flag proudly displayed in America should make people feel unwelcome. He asked if Gralapp had ever heard of Ellis Island and whether she thought an American flag should not have flown there, either. On the other hand, in this era of runaway political correctness, if the danger of giving offense to almost anyone over almost anything were to trump all other considerations, Gralapp's position might be defensible.

Except that the library had been showcasing, since Oct. 19, a display of 21 brightly-painted ceramic penises hanging from a clothesline in honor of Domestic Violence Awareness Month. The "artwork" was entitled Hanging 'Em Out to Dry. Now, who do you suppose 'Em might be? This couldn't be construed as tasteless male bashing, could it? Apparently someone felt that way. Last Saturday, compounding the city's embarrassment, a desperado plucked all 21 of the penises from their perch, removed them from the premises, and left in their place a small American flag and a calling card announcing that: "El Dildo Bandito was here." This latter-day Zorro, an upstanding family man with a 5-year-old daughter, then turned himself in to the authorities and surrendered the purloined penises. Only in Boulder.

Now here's the punch line, replete with smoking gun. During the penis display's tenure, library officials had posted a sign nearby warning patrons that they might be offended by it. Aha! So the danger of giving offense does not trump all other considerations. Gralapp has been hoist by her own petard. Boulder officials have once again been exposed as hypocrites. It's said that behind every double standard lies an unconfessed single standard: in this case, the liberal political agenda. Offensiveness, you see, is subjective. In the mindset of Boulder lefties, patriotic displays of the American flag are offensive, but crass penis-mongering in the cause of male bashing isn't.

In an earlier feeble attempt to save face, city officials assigned the damage control project to its public affairs director, Jana Petersen, tasking her to craft a more palatable position. Following a discussion of the ongoing incident on my radio program the other day, during which public outrage was evident, Petersen e-mailed me a "clarification of the facts." She claimed that Gralapp's initial decision was really based on the flag's excessive size, its location, and on the unavailability of smaller flags that might be placed in other locations. She even went so far as to invoke the good name of the American Legion, which, I was assured, had been contacted by library officials earlier in the week and was on the case looking for additional flags. Right. Conspicuously absent was any mention or defense of Gralapp's views on "objectivity" and the like. Yeah. That's the ticket. This is their revised story, and they're sticking to it.[52]

And stick to it they did. They waited out the storm, and eventually things began to settle down, at least in the media.

The trouble for me, however, was just beginning.

52. Mike Rosen, "Library Escapade Reveals PC Fallacy," *Rocky Mountain News*, November 20, 2001. Reprinted with permission of the *Rocky Mountain News*.

8

The Aftermath

As this story, and the city's strange handling of it, continued, I began to suspect that I was being ostracized
and isolated for my role in this. I figured that Marcelee
might have assumed that I was angry because of her
statements about Larry and his politics, and therefore I
must have been motivated to "rat" on her to the paper.
But I didn't.

It was obvious that I needed to prepare a defense, to
counter such a fallacy (or a phallucy, in this instance). I
knew that my only hope was to find out who really did
turn her in. How else could I prove that I didn't do it?
Shortly after the flag story broke, I retraced my steps to

the people on the staff that had been told about the flag after Marcelee had approved the display, but before she changed her mind. Every person on the maintenance and reference staffs denied that they had any contact with the *Daily Camera* reporter. I asked each person if his or her spouse may have been angry enough to do it, or one of their kids, and each one denied that. I even asked if they had talked about it in a public place like a restaurant, or even in front of an unsuspecting library customer, and again, everyone said that was not a possibility.

Ordinarily, given all of the bad press about the Boulder Public Library that had appeared in the past on Marcelee's watch (including the banning of the Nancy Drew and Hardy Boys books in the early 90's for being poorly written and racist, and the perplexing inclusion of Madonna's raunchy "Sex" book a few years later), everyone there shared at least a moderate disdain for any more such publicity, myself included. So, it was a total mystery to me who could have tipped off that reporter. Without proof of who did it, I knew that I would become the primary suspect.

And I became so quickly. People on the staff would come to me and say, "I heard it was you who talked to the newspaper," and I would deny it. To bolster my case, I would explain that it didn't even make sense that I would do that. First, the story initially came out that a group of employees wanted to hang up a flag, and the director said no. That's untrue on two counts; it was just me, and the director said yes at first. If I were inclined to leak what happened, I would have at least made sure they got the facts straight. Also, nearly three weeks passed between the day she changed her mind and the day the reporter called her. If I were inclined to turn her in because of anger, I would have done so much sooner than three weeks, as I was considerably cooled off by then. My credibility with the staff that I spoke to was very strong, and everyone seemed satisfied that it could not have been me.

But during that second week, after the Bandito struck and the news media attention was near its peak, I was asked to attend a meeting of around eight or nine staff members in the upstairs conference room, the first time I had been in the same room with Marcelee since the story broke. I don't recall the subject of the meeting, but Marcelee sat at the end of the long table, participating as usual, but with a reddish white face, nervous hands, and obvious stress. When someone asked, near the end of business, how she was handling it, she said, more than once, "I'm fighting for my job." She needed to leave quickly, apparently for another meeting with the city manager about the crisis. She did not make eye contact with me during the entire meeting, not even a fleeting glance. It was very uncomfortable. As it ended and people were departing a few at a time, I held back as Marcelee spoke to someone. As she was about to leave, I spoke up. "Marcelee, we haven't spoken since this flag thing broke out. Do you want to talk about what happened?" She turned to me, with an anger I had never seen before, and shouted out, "No! I want you to just STAY OUT OF IT." She then stormed out of the conference room.

That was the first time in thirteen years she had ever even come close to raising her voice to me. Other staffers were beginning to wonder what was going to happen if she did get fired over this. I pretty much avoided the tense scene in the Administration wing of offices for several weeks after that. The largely independent nature of my job responsibilities made that possible, including communicating when needed by brief emails.

I found out that Marcelee's first meeting with the five-member Library Commission after the flag flap was a stormy one. As a council-appointed citizen board that oversees policy and budget matters for the library, they demanded to know why they were not asked about the policy of banning American flags. Marcelee claimed that the denial of the flag display was a management decision, not a policy decision, and therefore did not require the Commission's input. Somehow, she survived that challenge.

When I was at a low point, several members of our family-like staff came to my rescue, offering their support. One of them came into my office one day to talk, and asked if I had heard the songs on the radio yet. What songs? About the flag flap and the dildos. Oh great. Somebody is now composing *songs* about this? But I was intrigued. Using my broadband connection to the internet, we found the link to them in Google, and there they were, ready to download. From a website created by Boulder resident Don Wrege, the songs were played frequently on KHOW radio to the Denver area commuters for several days. We closed the door and played the two tunes. It was a guilty pleasure, but while listening to these, I had my first genuine laugh in weeks.

Here are the lyrics to the first song, written and performed by Don Wrege to the tune of "Down in the West Texas Town of El Paso..."

El Dildo Bandido
to the tune of "El Paso" by Marty Robbins

Out in a town called Boulder Colorado
There was a public librarian there
She thought the American flag was insulting
But hanging penises so debonair

Young people gawked and asked their mothers questions
About the artwork called hung out to dry
Hanging a flag is no longer objective
Twenty-one penises though are all right

Then Peter Boyles got wind of the case
Media followed in stride---
A public employee thinks that our flag's offensive
Only in Boulder could she survive

So in anger
El Dildo Bandido felt he should take action
The situation had come to a head
He took the penises down from the display
Left an American flag instead

El Dildo Bandido is proud of his country
Proud of the freedom of speech that we share
But genitalia found hanging in public
Is out of place when the children are there

He staged a daring escape from the place
Out by the Canyon side—
Penises jangling he jumped into his car
Headed for Heatherwood where he resides

And the artist's
A psychology student who's seeking some answers
Maybe she'll find out why her art is sick

Then when the Boulder police did arrest him
El Dildo Bandido gladly confessed
Boulder Police had fin'ly found a suspect
Mainly because he gave them his address

Boulder's a place where even a nut case
Can be elected the Mayor—
But if you try to apply common sense
Buddy you don't have a chance or a prayer

And for now Bandido
Has been arrested and faces a court date
For his brave actions a veteran is tried
We should let Boulder officials hear our voice
Let them know that we are all on his side.[53]

53. Don Wrege, http://www.mediawhore.com ©2001. Used with permission.

Yeeeouch! I liked the imagery of the line, "Penises jangling he jumped into his car..." But there was more. This next one focused on the director, as follows:

Marcelee Gralapp
to the tune of "Eleanor Rigby" by Paul McCartney

Ahhh...look at all the dangling dildos
Ahhh...look at all the dangling dildos

Marcelee Gralapp
She caused a big flap when she refused to fly the flag
She's such a drag

Ben Nighthorse-Campbell
Wrote her a letter requesting that she change her mind
She still declined

All the dangling dildos
Anatomically correct
All the dangling dildos
Multicolored and erect

Changes her story
Now says the flag is too big to be hung in this place
With a straight face

Republic of Boulder
They support free speech if they agree with what you say
(Other)wise no way

What must she be thinking?
Well one thing leaves no doubt
(As) library director
It's time to check her out

Ahhh...look at all the dangling dildos
Ahhh...look at all the dangling dildos

Then Tom Tancredo
Drafted a bill that he knows won't see the light of day
But what the hey?

Marcelee Gralapp
Tries to defend her unpatriotic stance today
Please go away.

All the dangling dildos
Anatomically correct
All the dangling dildos
Multicolored and erect [54]

There were many items on the World Wide Web about this story, many of which can still be found by anyone with an interest.

I managed to endure the rest of that November at the library in relative isolation, while Marcelee surrounded herself with her usual supporters. I was busy with the final details of a contract for new coin-operated copy machines at all the branches, a project for the Library Foundation, and continued to deal with problems with the automated bookdrop. I also took several days off in December, hoping that the New Year would be a fresh start and a source of new hope.

My relationship with Marcelee and Larry was strictly business for the early part of 2002. But it was difficult to continue like that without clearing the air. Finally, on May 27, 2002, I decided to go into her office near the end of the day just to talk, like we used to. I wanted to assure her that I had nothing to do with delivering that flag story to the papers. She said that she was working on trying to get over it and still did not want to talk about what had happened. I believe that she was holding onto the belief that I turned her in, but there was nothing else that I could say, since I had no idea who leaked that story. So we talked about other things for a long time, including family matters. I could tell that she was a bit relieved and happy to be talking

54. Ibid.

again, and I was too. It wasn't quite just like old times, but it was a start.

But my troubles were not over. The rumors about my turning in the boss to the paper continued, despite my denials. The day after our meeting, I took a moment to type two letters, one to my Aunt in Boston, the other to an old college friend in West Virginia. They included news of my personal life and those of family members. Since I hadn't written to either in a long time, I also mentioned the highlights of the flag flap, and included some internet links to the story. Without mentioning Larry, I told them about how Marcelee approved the flag, about our afternoon meeting days later, and how she changed her mind. I wrote to my Aunt, "...some of her liberal friends, who view the flag as some sort of Republican call to war, got to her and she changed her mind. But too many people knew about it already, and somebody called the local paper. It exploded after that..."

Well, I typed these in my office at lunchtime, and for one of them, I hit the "print" icon, and nothing came out of my often unreliable, networked office printer. Unsure why it didn't go, I used the drop down menu, printed it that way, and it worked. I didn't think much of it. Many months later, I learned that the first letter had printed upstairs, in the shared Administration printer. I was always finding personal stuff in that printer from all kinds of people, and the custom was to just leave it there, or set it to one side. But I was told of someone on the Administration staff that found my letter, and took it directly to Marcelee's office to give it to her as "proof" that I was the one who turned her in to the press. I found out from a friend of Marcelee's more than a year later that she was showing this letter to people as proof of my disloyalty. The trouble was that there was nothing in that letter that said any such thing.

But before I knew this, something else happened shortly thereafter. On June 14, 2002, Marcelee summoned me to her office. Saying, "I know you've been having trouble with [Larry]," she announced that I would no longer be reporting to him, but to Priscilla, the branch manager. Priscilla and I had a kind of détente relationship, able to work together without too much friction because we were on equal footing. This change was clearly not going to work, and I saw it as punishment and a demotion. "This is not a demotion," Marcelee insisted, but a reflection of the importance of the new bookdrop. But my role in the bookdrop project was finishing up, with the maintenance duties going to others. A coworker said having to report to Priscilla was "worse than being fired on the spot." I suddenly found myself at the bottom of the organizational chart in Administration. This was outrageous.

I contemplated quitting over this, and I made sure she knew it. Word got around, and I understand that some of the librarians met with her to complain about what she decided, saying they couldn't function without my doing all the things I did for them. But Marcelee wouldn't budge. As it turned out, I was able to deal with Priscilla more easily than I had imagined, and the day to day problems were manageable. But I had the distinct feeling that I was being marginalized there. I continued to work Saturdays and take Mondays off, usually going on Monday hikes that summer in the Indian Peaks Wilderness west of Boulder. I found that hikes of several miles, above eleven thousand feet did wonders to clear my head and ease my frustrations.

Sometime in August, Marcelee began telling people that she was going to retire early the next year, 2003. She had been there for forty three years, and was now in her seventies.

So who was going to replace the legendary, always-present Marcelee? Dare I even think it—me, perhaps? Stay tuned.

9

Susan Honstein (left) and Marcelee (right)

Going for the Top Job

A long time ago, probably around 1990 or so, I was listening to Marcelee talking about her tactics to get a North Boulder branch library, which would be her fifth. She would stir up public discussions about the where, how and when, telling me that if you did that often enough, no one would ever go back and ask the "why." It would take on a life of its own, and the council would have to find a way to fund it. This was just as the finishing work on the huge new downtown library was underway. She was already in her sixties at that point. So I asked her, "Marcelee, are you *ever* going to retire?" While anyone else would reply "someday," or "I'm thinking about it," she said in a very serious tone, "I'm not leaving here until I'm in a sufficiently powerful position to *name my own successor*." I was aghast, replying, "But that will be up to whoever the city manager is at the time, not you." She replied, very matter-of-factly, "When the time comes, that won't matter."

In August, 2002, with talk of her retirement in less than a year, the whole place was abuzz about what would happen. There was speculation that she wanted Larry to be the heir to the throne. That was not a popular choice among many of us, to say the least. And I don't think Larry wanted the job anyway.

In September, a few staff members approached me and encouraged me to compete for the director job. At first I thought it was an impossible dream. I was not a librarian but an MBA, and I was a man in an almost entirely female hierarchy. But the idea grew on me. I even drew up a list of my selling points and a sizing up of my few internal competitors. Maybe I could pull this off.

I knew that library system inside and out. I knew all the people, their good and bad points, and how to deal with them. I held a strong connection to the town, and a strong love of the institution, despite all of the flag related abuse. I had written a well-received master plan; I would be the logical choice to implement it. I had a unique plan to finally get a north branch without raising taxes, and a way to reduce the budget without layoffs. I could introduce more science programs for children and adults, in a community that probably has far more working scientists than artists. I could combine the best attributes of Marcelee's management style without any of her drawbacks. I could maintain policies that were responsive to everyone in our community without having to resort to the extremes of political correctness. I could moderate the library's image of fostering an extreme feminist agenda, throw out the cronyism, restore honesty and trust with the staff, and make the library more responsive to the needs of everyone. This could work. This could be great.

I even fantasized about getting the job, then immediately hanging the famous 10' × 15' American flag in the coneoid, at long last, with a sign saying "Under New Management." But that would be too harsh. Perhaps a more politically correct sign would be, "As your new library director, this flag will be on a temporary display as a belated tribute to the victims of 9/11, and as a celebration of the freedoms we enjoy in this country to come inside and read whatever we please. In the event that anyone is offended by the sight of our flag, the South Boulder branch will remain a flag-free alternative for the duration." I may never have carried it out, but it was a nice thought.

Then there was a major surprise. Larry took an early retirement package, and vanished. Marcelee seemed stunned by this change of plans. When I talked to her about who would now replace her, her attitude was quite lax. "I don't care," she said, in an uncharacteristic, defeatist attitude, only that she was going to retire herself on schedule. But she also said that the city was going to have to conduct a thorough, nationwide search for a highly qualified director to take her place. That seemed a bit grandiose to me, given that she was the head of the tiny children's room years earlier when she got the job. So, if she didn't have anyone in mind internally to push through, perhaps I had a chance after all.

The city manager formed a committee to study what was needed in a new director, and the qualifications that would be required. I knew from looking at ads in trade magazines like *Library Journal* that most library director applicants must have an MLS degree, or

Masters in Library Science, to apply. But I found recent examples where that was not the case, mostly in library systems much larger than ours. I knew that my fifteen years of administration experience was more than sufficient. Marcelee herself was a long time critic of the MLS requirement for library directors, not for the education they receive, but for the kind of person who is attracted to the degree program. "They want to help Mrs. Jones find her book," she would say, not the sort who would be good at dealing with boards, city councils, budgets, facilities, or labor issues.

So, I had to be sure the MLS did not become a mandatory requirement for the Boulder job if I was to stand a chance.

I knew one of the members of that committee, a former library commissioner who was very friendly. I ran into her at the local supermarket. Out of the blue, she said, "Chris, why don't *you* apply?" I said I was thinking about it, and would like to speak to her about my ideas. We met at her home on a Saturday morning in January, 2003 where I presented my case. I argued about why an MLS should not be a requirement, and got her to agree with me and pledge her support for my candidacy. She promised to make the same arguments to the committee. After her next meeting, she said they agreed to drop the MLS requirement, but only after some lively and lengthy arguments. So, I got past that potential stopper. Only later did I realize that I had opened the door for another non-MLS internal candidate. More on that later.

Just before Marcelee retired, she appointed a six-member "interim team" to run the library, instead of an interim director. Liz Abbott was appointed as the head of that team. The library was now being run by committee. I was not chosen to be on that team, and am unaware if my name ever even came up. Five of the six people were women, and only one was a librarian. Marcelee had a strong affinity for getting women into as many top jobs in the city as she could, and I would never do. And I'm sure she still had bad feelings about her belief of my disloyalty over the flag flap leak. I knew that not having her on my side would be a serious impediment.

In February, I also checked with an MLS-holding librarian in our children's department who knew about the state laws that pertain to libraries. I needed to know if Colorado had an MLS requirement in the law for library directors, as many states do. She said there was talk of passing such a law, but none was in effect yet. Another stopper was dodged.

Meanwhile, Ron Secrist, the city manager who presided over the flag flap and dildo episodes, announced that he was leaving the city to work for a local hospital foundation. The council was going through a search process for his replacement. I remember that one female council member complained that none of the six finalists were women. They selected Frank Bruno, who had been a deputy city manager in Fort Collins, north of Boulder. So, Boulder chose someone who had never actually been a city manager before, at a time when our old Crossroads shopping mall was shutting down because of competition in surrounding cities, resulting in a sharp decline in sales tax receipts. Bruno began during the last week of February, and I had a brief introduction at a reception in the library gallery, steps away from where the penises had hung a year earlier.

Marcelee's retirement party, held in the library art gallery, was on March 3, 2003. The dildos were not invited back for the event. The catered party went on for several hours, with hundreds of people coming in, each waiting in a sort of receiving line to pay their respects. It was also the official party for the earlier retirement of

Larry, who made an appearance. Manager Frank Bruno, looking quite nervous, presided over the presentations. When announcing Larry's departure, he said that Larry had generously donated some of his vacation pay to purchase computers for a group of children in South America. The crowd applauded.

I was still debating the idea of going for the director job in my own mind. I remember the exact moment I made the final decision to proceed. I was doing some spring skiing on the East Wall at Arapahoe Basin, an impossibly steep, ungroomed slope located far above treeline and reached by a long traversing trail. At some point, you have to screw up your courage to jump off the safe traverse and do a free fall down the steep slope. Was I ready to take the plunge? For the director job AND this challenging descent? That was it—I was. I jumped forward, carved a heroic high speed turn and screamed down that mountain, legs burning, out of breath. I did it. If I could do that, I was now sure that I was up to the director challenge too. Some of us do things like that in Colorado.

The city manager put Susan Honstein, a long time employee in human resources, in charge of the formal director search. I was concerned about her impartiality, as she, Marcelee and Elizabeth Abbott were all old friends. But Liz, who Marcelee had put as the head of the Management Team, was insisting that she was not an applicant. I didn't see anyone else on the staff who could be a viable candidate, so it appeared to be me versus an outsider that a headhunter would bring in.

Meanwhile, the forecasts for the city's revenue were grim, and Bruno was making plans for potentially deep budget cuts and layoffs. The library team had to draw up different budget scenarios, depending on how deep the cuts would have to be. A ballot issue to extend an expiring sales tax and spare most of the jobs would be decided in November, but they had to be prepared in case the issue failed, resulting in the deepest cuts.

On May 7, I was summoned to the Administration offices, where Liz, Priscilla, and Ray Ingraham, the head of the computer department, announced that my job was being downsized as of the end of the year. I was stunned. They refused to say who else was affected. I asked if the job might be saved if the tax extension passes, and they said no. I was shocked, but realized that the urgency of my director bid was now paramount. The next day, Frank Bruno held a presentation in the city council chambers for anyone on the city staff who wanted to hear details about the layoffs, so I attended. He referred to his budget cutting plan as "turning the ship." I kept thinking how I was the one being made to walk the plank.

But I seized on an opportunity that he announced that very day. He called it his "Displaced Employee Policy." It was later sent out by email to everyone on the layoff list. It said that if any city job opening occurs for the next two years, the hiring supervisor must first advertise the job only to the people on the displaced list. Whoever applies must then be interviewed by the supervisor, and given the job offer if they meet the more relaxed standard of being a "reasonable fit for the job," instead of the best possible fit. It even went so far as to say that if a candidate was not a reasonable fit but could become one with some training, they would still get the offer.

Hey, this was great. I was much more than just a reasonable fit, and since the director would report to Bruno himself, he would have to interview me before any candidates that a headhunter would provide. In fact, his policy said the supervisor cannot even advertise the job to other city staff or outside candidates until the displaced employee is considered and a yes/no decision made. I intended to take full advantage of this new rule. I was still suspicious that Liz Abbot was going to apply, and this gave me a big edge over her, because she was in no danger of being laid off. I was just as qualified, if not more so.

Meanwhile, Susan Honstein was taking a long time just to select a headhunter firm for the search, and refused to create a job description before one was chosen. I was walking into the library one morning and ran into Susan. She asked if I had photographs of the library that she could use for the library director recruiting brochure. I had a conflict of interest, of course. I didn't want to attract more competition with my best photos. But I agreed, and sent her several by email, insisting on a photo credit in her brochure. I asked her how the headhunter selection was coming, and she said that it was down to a few firms. But she said she would probably go with someone they had used before. Now, that was puzzling. We haven't replaced our library director in nearly forty years. I said, "So, you're not going to use one that specializes in recruiting library directors?" She looked surprised, and asked, "Do you know of one?" Isn't that her job to know that? I knew that such firms existed, but nothing specific. And the competition thing came to mind again. "Um, no." I got out of that conversation.

I later found out that someone on our reference staff sent Susan a list of the best known national recruiters who specialize in library directors, but as it turned out, it did nothing to alter her plans.

There were many days when I saw Susan spending hours in Liz Abbott's office, with the door closed. Meanwhile, Judy Volc, the beloved and well known children's librarian who had been there for more than thirty years, also retired. During Judy's farewell party on June 20th, held on the steps of the children's garden, Marcelee got up to say a few words. She spoke at length about how much she enjoyed her own retirement, never once mentioning Judy. After the speeches, Susan Honstein approached me to encourage me to apply for a job opening in the parks department, managing their detailed budgets. I smelled a rat instantly. I figured that if I took that job, I would no longer be "displaced" and she could get me out of the competition for the director spot. I told her my primary interest was the library director job. She continued to push the parks option, saying that I could still apply for "that other one," unable to even say it out loud. Well, I found out that there had been several people in that parks job over a short period of years, and I was advised by someone I trusted to avoid it. The library director job was where I belonged.

My next task was to do the impossible, to win over Marcelee. I paid her a visit at her home, where we sat at her dining room table. After some small talk, I told her that her team had decided to do away with my job. Marcelee claimed that she didn't know that, and didn't look at all surprised. I then said I was serious about applying for her old job. She looked away, smiling, and said, "We'll have to find something else for you to do next year."

So, I made my point. I told Marcelee that if the city searches the country for this super qualified director that she insists must fill her shoes, that person is going to want to form the library in his or her own image, not hers. That kind of person isn't going to welcome a lot of suggestions from the retired director. Marcelee looked worried, as if she hadn't thought of that. Was I making progress? I decided to continue with my line of reasoning. "And with the declining budget, that director is going to look over all of those art programs you built into the budget over many years, and ask if we are a library or an art center, and start cutting." That got her attention. I was pretty sure I didn't win her over, but at least got her to think.

I was collecting letters of recommendation at that time from some high profile people. Although I was a bit shy about asking, everyone came through with strong endorsements. A former Boulder city manager said, "Chris is an outstanding manager," calling me "exceptionally bright, articulate and dedicated" and that "he understands the politics without being part of them." A former chief financial officer of a Denver hospital said that I was "that rare soul who thrives in the spheres both of strategic planning and of real-world operation." An ex-library commissioner cited "Mr. Power's integrity and ethics," and that, "The welfare of the library and its employees has always served as his guide in decision-making and planning." Judy Volc, the former children's librarian, wrote, "I believe that Chris would be an outstanding library and arts director for Boulder." A library director from another state wrote, "I have found him to be knowledgeable in the area of library design, services and administration." And Sally McVey, who hired me at the Boulder Public Library back in 1988, wrote, "I believed that Chris would be running some big corporation by now, with his background. But he has a real commitment to that library that he helped to build." These letters made me blush; they provided a big boost to my confidence and determination.

But one of my requests for a letter was declined. That person explained that he respected my skills and integrity, but had already written a recommendation for someone else. That turned out to be Liz Abbott. She was still denying that she was in the running at that point. I sensed trouble.

10

The library's 7-person administration staff, and
one other, March, 2003. Given the city's passion
for diversity, guess which one got the boot?

Abuse of Power

On May 30, 2003, before Judy Volc's farewell party, I
sent an email to Susan Honstein, officially informing her of my intention to apply for the director job. I
specifically said that I would be applying as a displaced
employee. Instead of scheduling the interview, she replied
that Frank Bruno needed to think about the job requirements and how to proceed.

By August, a recruiter was finally chosen, a "headhunter" from California. According to the firm's website,
Boulder was their only non-California client, and they
appeared to do searches for city managers, planning directors and the like, and certainly did not specialize in

the recruitment of library directors. I found out that this firm had been used a year earlier by Susan to recruit the new parks director, Jan Geden, so she did choose a firm she had used before, not a library director specialist.

The job description was finally posted for displaced employees on our email system, and I had twenty four hours to apply. I walked the application over to human resources and had them stamp it with the day and time. As expected, I was the only displaced applicant. I was expecting my interview with Bruno, but that didn't happen. Instead, on August 22, the top man in this headhunter firm came to Boulder from California to interview me, in a city hall conference room. I thought it went very well. After nearly two hours, I asked about the process. He had the displaced policy printout in front of him, with some sentences marked with a yellow highlighter pen.

Choosing his words carefully, he said that they didn't yet know how the process was going to go, but that they might "open it up" to outside applicants. I wanted to argue with him, but again, needed to be polite and not rock any boats. I explained that I was going to lose my old job in just a few months, and I needed to know how realistic this was. When questioned, he confirmed that I met the requirements, and that I was a "strong contender" for the job. When I pressed for details about the displaced policy, he only said that an inside candidate has a natural advantage over anyone from outside. I realized that he probably had an interest in opening this up to outsiders, to maximize his fees. This was not going well for me. I asked him if I would be a finalist if he opens it up to others. He jumped at the reply, and assured me that I would "definitely" be a finalist.

That weekend, he left a voice mail message, saying that because of my lack of experience as a library director, they decided to open it up to other candidates.

So, a waiting game began, as he and Susan conducted their unusually long search. On September 14, there was a dedication ceremony at the main library that brought Marcelee back from retirement. Her friends and some former and current staff attended. As I was talking to one staff member, who was encouraging me to press for the director job, Larry came walking in, headed for Marcelee's entourage. As he passed, he gave me a long, cold stare. What was that about? It didn't bother me. He was gone, and I didn't want his endorsement.

On September 28, an article in the *Daily Camera* left the city staff all abuzz for weeks. Columnist Jon Caldera published the names, titles and salaries of city employees making over $80,000 per year. The figures, from 2003, included all benefit costs, not just salaries, and included termination pay for a few who left the city that year. Actual salaries were probably about 20 percent less. But it shattered the myth that our top librarians and other city staff were underpaid. Marcelee cost the city $144,482 per year, while Larry was $108,489, and Susan Honstein was $98,382. Even Priscilla was reported to cost $93,486. He also mentioned that the median household income in Boulder was $44,748, and that Colorado's governor made $90,000.[55] I did not make the list.

So, after minimal advertising by the headhunter, they settled on five finalists in November, and I was one of them. They would not disclose to me or to anyone else who the others were. The end of my fifteen-year job was coming up fast. It came out just before the interviews that Liz Abbott was a finalist after all. I was not surprised.

It was later revealed in the paper that there were only *thirty two* applicants, for a job that should have attracted a few hundred. I spoke to a library director in

55. Jon Caldera, "Boulder's city employees are doing very, very well," *Daily Camera*, September 28, 2003.

Michigan who is active in the Public Library Association and had her ear to the ground on key director openings. "No one is talking about the Boulder job," she told me, speculating that it wasn't properly advertised. This low application rate seemed to support my suspicions that Susan and her headhunter might be trying to limit competition for Liz.

Monday, December 8, 2003 was the first day of interviews. The plan was for each of the five finalists to be interviewed by Bruno, then the Library Team. The field would be narrowed to three, to continue interviews the next day. Then Bruno would decide that evening.

On the Friday before the interview, I spoke to the woman in the headhunter's office in California who was handling the scheduling. I happened to ask if my letters of reference, handed to the headhunter during my August interview, had been sent to Bruno. She said she never saw them, and would have known if they had been sent with my other application materials. So what happened to them? Since Bruno didn't know me at all, those glowing letters of reference were crucial to making my case as a viable candidate for this job.

So I got the name of Bruno's secretary, who was very nice and probably knew nothing about what was going on. I told her that I had a stack of original letters of reference that he needed to see before Monday. She assured me that she would place them in his hands before then, so I rushed over there and gave her the letters.

I had to go first, at 8:00 Monday morning, after a night of little sleep. I was trying to be confident, but knowing that it was either this or unemployment created intense pressure that none of the other finalists had to face. I was granted just fifteen minutes to meet Bruno, which worked out to one minute for each year that I worked for the library. Susan Honstein and her headhunter friend sat across the table, watching. There was no time to make my pitch at all, and I expressed my eagerness to talk to him in more detail. Then I was taken to a conference room, where I was asked prepared questions by four of his other department heads, including the police chief, one of the public works officials, the parks director, and Jana Peterson, the person who distributed all of that spin to the media about the flag and dildos two years earlier and was subsequently promoted to assistant city manager. None of the questions had anything to do with the library, being more general management topics. But it seemed to go well. At the end, I reminded the group that I was a displaced employee, about to lose my job of fifteen years, and hoped that would be a major consideration. The group looked uncomfortable about that, perhaps because some of them had to lay off people themselves.

Then I had to walk over to the library and face forty five minutes of questions from the library management team. This was the same group that was about to lay me off. It was very tense. When the session ended, I walked out and went home, exhausted. But I assured myself that, as a displaced internal applicant, I would almost certainly make it to the next round.

Wrong. Bruno phoned late that day, with "bad news." I was crushed, and asked why. He seemed to be in a hurry to get off of the phone and would only say that they identified three others who would "better serve the long term interests of the library," and ended the call abruptly. He didn't even know me, or take the time to act on his own policy for displaced employees. That hurt.

The crushing reality of what was now going to happen hit me, and I felt sick. In fact, I called in sick for the remainder of that week, coming in during the evenings to begin packing up my office stuff.

The next day, the three finalists were interviewed. Liz was one of them. The other two were unidentified. The paper mentioned the libraries they came from, one in California, the other in New York. They had to take turns answering questions from the staff in the auditorium, and the feedback I got was that none of the candidates seemed particularly strong for various reasons.

There was no white smoke coming from the chimneys of city hall that evening, as planned. I made a phone call to Marcelee that turned out to be my last. I told her what happened, and she didn't seem at all surprised. I told her that there could well be some legal action on my part against the city because of the policy violations. That could drag her out of retirement, and her response took me by surprise. "You do whatever you have to do, Chris. I'm outta there." She didn't seem to care.

More than a week went by without a decision. I was told that Bruno was sent a letter from the library management team, complaining about the choice of candidates. They expected a more impressive list, and were concerned that the search was not handled properly. The letter was ineffective; Bruno refused to alter his course.

On December 18, my next-to-last day, the announcement was finally made by email. Bruno picked Liz Abbott, the budget analyst. This was one of the people who was said to have talked Marcelee out of hanging that American flag after 9/11. It looked to me like Marcelee was determined to repay that loyalty. That headhunter "opened up" the process to Liz and others because of my lack of experience as a director, and after spending about $50,000 on his services and travel for finalists during a budget crisis, who did they pick? Someone who also lacked director experience and the MLS degree. Members of the staff came by my office while I was packing to express their anger and sympathy. One staff member said to me, "This has Marcelee's fingerprints all over it."

About two weeks later, I got another surprise. After nearly two decades with the city, Susan Honstein announced that she was leaving to take a new job in Arizona. The staff rumors abounded, some fearing she might have tampered with this process as her final favor to Marcelee and Liz. Given the timing, it seems entirely possible that she had her job offer in hand before the director interviews. It was looking like the Old Girl's Club had closed ranks, eliminated the competition, and maintained their dominance and power.

After the tax extension passed in the November election and most of the planned cuts were restored, I found out that I was the *only* member of the library staff who was laid off.

People familiar with the flag/dildo story often asked me, "So whatever became of the big flag?" Good question. I came across the flag, in its original box, while cleaning out my office just before my job was terminated. What would I do with it? That big ol' flag and I had a unique bond, and I was very fond of it. I certainly didn't want this group to ever fly it at that library, having had all the hypocrisy I could stand. But the city taxpayers paid for it, so I couldn't take it with me.

On the Sunday before my layoff, I came down to my office to continue the sorting and packing. On the way in, I saw a friend sitting at a table on the indoor bridge by the espresso bar. I suddenly had an idea. I asked if he would take my picture in front of the library with my camera as I held the flag. "I'm in!" he replied. I got some strange looks from some passing library patrons as I stood there with the partially unfolded 10' × 15' American flag while my friend snapped some pictures.

When I returned to my office, another idea came to me. I had to leave the flag in the building, but I was under no obligation to disclose *where*. So I packed it very carefully, and hid it in a part of the building they may not find until the next renovation, perhaps decades from now. It was a small act of rebellion, but I needed to do something to express my rage. The flag remains safely hidden, despite reports from staff that a member of the management team was hunting for it after my departure.

My last day was December 19, ironically, Liz Abbott's first day as director. It was also just six days before Christmas. That morning, I had to go to the city attorney's office to collect my final paycheck, including a payoff of my accrued vacation and sick leave. The taxes and withholdings took more than half. I was also offered a few thousand more in severance pay, but only if I would sign a document releasing them from legal liability, which I refused. I could have used the money, certainly, but they could not buy my silence. I wanted my options open.

Three of my friends on the staff, who really wanted me to be their new leader, took me to lunch to say goodbye. They told me that Marcelee and Liz were having a celebratory lunch down the street at the same time.

I was still packing up my things that final afternoon when the "Old Girls" came into my office. I found out that they had just been celebrating Liz's victory upstairs. I was cornered, and really didn't want to face them, or endure any more knives in my back. They gave me a pen that I ended up never using, and each insisted on a hug. What a nightmare. On my final trip across the bridge carrying items to my car, I passed Ray Ingraham, one of the team members who voted for my ouster. He had a grin on his face, and said, 'Do you want any help?" "You've done quite enough," I thought, and brushed by him. I left my keys and security card on my desk, like I was checking out of a cheap motel, so as to avoid Priscilla and any of her typically callous remarks. I took a last look around, suspecting that I wouldn't want to come into that library ever again. I walked out of the art gallery into the cold December air and got into my car, parked next to those ten American flags on the poles that stretched toward city hall, and drove away.

But hold on...this story is not over yet. Something incredible happened the very next day.

11

Sparky the Firedog

Flag Flap's "Deep Throat" Revealed

That first post-layoff weekend was very hard. I was sleeping too much, had no appetite, and felt very depressed, just days before Christmas. The lights and decorations on the Pearl Street Mall brought me no joy. I didn't feel like celebrating Kwanzaa either. I felt like a hit and run victim. What just happened? Was it possible that Marcelee was seeking her revenge on me, all because of my supposed role in that blemish on her record, the flag flap? It continued to annoy me that I never knew who really did turn her in, but it could have been anyone. As I already explained, my previous investigation of suspects turned up nothing. It remained a mystery for two years.

That weekend, I got a call from a friend named Hazel Cowen, wanting to express her sympathy. Hazel was an elderly woman with curly white hair, a former New Yorker who retained the accent, who used to be a volunteer reader every Wednesday morning in the children's room. Her sidekick during those readings was a member of the fire department named, "Sparky the Firedog," who wore a Dalmatian costume and a fireman's coat and helmet. Someone would speak to the adorable tots about fire safety as Sparky did a little dance. Sparky and Hazel were a big hit with Boulder's littlest library patrons and their mothers. I almost got a chance to substitute for Sparky one day, which might have been fun, but it didn't work out.

Hazel would start her morning of volunteering each week over coffee by the library's espresso shop, and I got to know her, long before the flag flap, while waiting for my daily cup. I always believed in taking some time to talk to the library's wonderful group of volunteers. She really believed that becoming the new director was my destiny.

During her phone call, she once again expressed her anger toward Marcelee and her banishment of the American flag. I told her that I really wished I knew how the paper found out about all of that, and to my complete astonishment, Hazel *confessed*. Here's what happened.

On the day that Marcelee sent me her email giving me the go-ahead on the flag, I showed a color copy of the flag description from Ebay to Hazel and described my plan to hang it in the entryway, knowing that she would approve. She was so pleased with the idea that she offered to pay for half. I assured her that the city would pay for it, but was grateful for her offer. Of course, the following week when she asked when it would arrive, I had to break the news that Marcelee had changed her mind and the flag wouldn't be hung after all. Hazel seemed about as upset as anyone else. Three weeks later, when all hell broke loose after the first newspaper article, I asked Hazel if she had contacted the reporter, and she denied it. That was the truth.

But in that pre-Christmas phone call two years later, Hazel explained that she was so mad about Marcelee's decision to ban the flag that she told her neighbor all about it. As an example of how small this town can still be, both Marcelee and I know Hazel's neighbor. Equally upset by the news, the neighbor then told her husband, who is the editorial page editor at the *Daily Camera*. I couldn't believe it. Because I knew this neighbor of Hazel's, I called her right away for confirmation. I had to hear this from her.

It was true. The neighbor explained that she normally never passes along information that she hears to her husband, but this flag-banning matter was just too much. She knew that a *Camera* reporter, Greg Avery, was working on a story about flags around Boulder, and suggested to her husband that he ask the reporter to call the library to inquire why a flag display request had been turned down.

In 2005, while investigating the matter for this book, I asked that editor at the *Daily Camera*, Steve Millard, to confirm this sequence of events and exonerate me once and for all from blame. He said that my description of the source coming from Hazel and his wife "is essentially correct," and he provided this written response:

> Chris—I've talked with Greg Avery, and our recollections are similar. You did not "leak" the story to the *Camera*, and neither of us ever spoke to you. In October of 2001, Greg was working on a broader story about the display of American flags

in Boulder after 9/11. I was not Greg's editor and had no direct control over his story; I simply told him what I knew about the library and suggested that he might want to check it out. He agreed—and the rest, as they say, is history.[56]

So, the pieces were falling into place. Word of the denied flag display went from me to Hazel (right after the flag display had been approved), then from Hazel to her neighbor (after the flag ban), then to the neighbor's husband the editor, and finally to the reporter, who then interviewed Marcelee. That sequence of communications also explains the three week lag between the decision to ban the flag and the reporter's phone call, and the inaccuracies that evolved about a "group" of employees wanting to fly the flag and the director's immediate denial of the request.

In that phone call to Hazel's neighbor, I explained that, although I very well might have done the same thing if someone had given me such inflammatory information, her doing so probably cost me a promotion and my old job, leaving me unemployed. I also explained that I suspected that Marcelee had been trying to destroy my reputation around town for the past two years by propagating this rumor of my guilt, unjustly. I asked this neighbor of Hazel's at the time if she would be willing to call Marcelee to confess, or even just drop a note in the mail. She refused both options. Why? "Because I *hate* that woman." Oh great.

Hazel the senior citizen volunteer appeared on Denver television for a few seconds in the early days of the flag flap. As she was leaving the library, she was stopped by a reporter with a camera crew. She said that she was

---

56. Steve Millard, editorial page editor for the *Daily Camera*, e-mail message to author, December 15, 2005.

proud of the American flag and that it should be on display. She told me that as she was speaking in front of the camera, she saw Marcelee just inside the library doors, "hiding in the background."

Sometime after that interview, Hazel picked up one of the library calendars and was shocked to see that her beloved story hour was being cancelled and replaced with a program called Creek Walk, where the youngsters would be led on a walk along Boulder Creek by someone on the staff. Hazel's job was gone. She said that she was not told beforehand, and resented finding out that way, after nine years of volunteer work there. She quickly began reading to children at Boulder Community Hospital instead, and told me that she refuses to set foot in the Boulder Public Library again. She is now convinced that her appearance on TV supporting the flag as Marcelee watched had something to do with her dismissal.

Hazel had one other interesting story from those days. About a year after the flag/dildo flap, she phoned an 800 number to order more checks from her bank. When Hazel asked where the girl on the other end of the line was, she was told, "Texas." When Boulder was mentioned, the Texas operator said, "Oh, you're from that place that banned the flag!" She told Hazel that everyone in her office was talking about it at the time and was very upset, but also amused by the related stories about the artwork. It's another example of how far-reaching the story became, and how people still remembered it.

Hazel felt terrible that she might have had any role in what happened to me. We continued to meet for coffee after that, and became good friends. Yes, she indirectly leaked this story to the press and started a lot of trouble, but how could I stay mad at this grandmotherly figure that stood up for the American flag and used to read to the children along with Sparky the Fire Dog?

And where else but Boulder could such a tragically weird thing happen? So, at long last, at least I knew. I could now prove that Marcelee had blamed the wrong guy, but it was too late. The damage was done. Armed with this new information, could I obtain any justice? We shall see.

12

The Investigation

I didn't think I would ever have as sad a Christmas as the one after my Mother died exactly ten months before the 9/11 attacks, and the flag/dildo mess thereafter. But this one right after the layoff, and Hazel's confession, came close. And when it was over, I realized that I had no job to go back to. And yet, I also began to realize that it was quite a relief not to have to go back there.

I really needed to get out of Boulder for a few days. So I got a cheap airline ticket and went to Boston to visit the Power relatives. There were American flags all over Boston, flying in the cold January wind, and some suburban gas stations were covered with hundreds of them.

If I needed to get away from American flags, I picked the wrong city. I spent an evening telling my 80-year-old Aunt Ruth this whole story, and she encouraged me to stand up for myself. In her wonderful Bostonian accent, she declared, "Don't let the *baaas-teds* win!"

So when I returned, I decided to pursue the formal grievance process for management employees with the city over my dismissal and the suspicious director search, as I intended to get some answers. I wrote a letter to the head of human resources to ask for an investigation, the required first step. Over the holidays, the HR director left that position and was replaced with an interim director, Roy Wallace. He reviewed the recruitment materials and interviewed Frank Bruno and the headhunter.

In a written response from Wallace, Bruno said that while he did receive input from the library team, other department heads and the library commissioners, "any weight given to other's opinions was somewhat minimal" and was only used as "background information" to confirm his own thinking, "without any undue influence" on his choice. I'm sure all of those people will be happy to hear that.

The California headhunter was now giving a very different story about our first interview. Wallace claimed the displaced policy was a "generic policy," and that the recruitment of directors differs in significant ways. But the policy, in fact, mentioned no such exceptions. They claim that I was interviewed first, as the policy required. But it was by that outside headhunter, not the hiring supervisor. He is on record in the investigation as saying that he told me in the interview, as a displaced employee, that I would be "a likely finalist." What happened to "strong contender?" He said he explained to me that with my qualifications, if it were not for my status as a displaced employee, I would not have been a finalist at all.

But that would have been true for Liz Abbot and her lack of qualifications as well, and she got the job.

The next step in the city's process was to have a hearing with an independent third party presiding, which I requested. These kinds of hearings were quite common. But that final part of due process never happened. It was blocked by Bruno himself. He sent a letter to me dated February 9, 2004, saying that as a witness in this case, "I would not want to place someone subordinate to me in the role of reviewing my decision." He would also not allow my suggestion of an outside, independent officer to resolve the problem, saying that it would set a bad precedent (I later learned that the use of a third party by the city had been done in the past). So he decided to "declare an exception to the policy and skip this final step." He was asking for a lawsuit. Since the city council who hired him is not allowed to be involved in personnel matters, he apparently answers to no one but the courts.

I got a call the morning after my first consultation with a Boulder labor attorney. In the morning paper, it had been announced that the former head of a now defunct department, who was also on the list to be laid off, had been hired by Bruno for a new, high-level job reporting to him. The story in the paper explained that this person was hired under the city's displaced employee policy, and quoted Bruno as following that policy to justify the hiring without any other interviews or outside advertising or recruitment. This attorney called me the first thing that morning, confused. He asked me why Frank chose to follow his displaced policy in this case but not mine. Bingo. Now he understood. "Holy shit, what is it with this guy?" the lawyer asked, incredulously. This attorney was stunned that Bruno chose to cut it off without the required final hearing.

Meanwhile, I began applying for other jobs. I knew

it would not be easy to start over outside of government, even though I really wanted to after what the city of Boulder put me through. But local employers were suffering from businesses leaving Boulder, and resented the city's role in that. Having "City of Boulder" on my resume was no selling point. I was being painted with the same, broad brush as the people who I believe pushed me out for wanting to fly the flag. I began networking with everyone I knew, and found a lack of hiring interest everywhere.

There was one bright spot. I found an advertised opening for a library director in the little but prosperous town of Basalt, Colorado, about fifteen miles down the Roaring Fork valley from Aspen. I applied, and despite the California headhunter's "official" assessment of my poor qualifications to be a library director, became one of four finalists for Basalt. I arrived two days early, to do some fantastic February skiing in Aspen. The lengthy interview by their board went well. Someone else was chosen, but I was told they were very impressed with me, and feared that with my background, I wouldn't stay. The job paid less than I made in Boulder, and the cost of living was much higher. Perhaps they were seeking a more traditional librarian and it wasn't a good fit, but I was very happy to be chosen as a finalist after the dreadful Boulder experience.

I also wondered about the other two unidentified finalists for the Boulder job. I phoned the one from California, who I found on Google in seconds. She was remarkably candid, saying that she was trying to "forget it" and was "perplexed" by the final choice. She told me she suspected that the process was rigged when she walked into the library team interview. She saw on the website beforehand that there were six interim members on that team, but counted only five at the table. She said she instantly knew the missing one was going to get it. "Why did they put so many people through so much trouble when they already knew?" I assured her that she was better off where she was. I was unable to locate the other candidate.

Only five months after my layoff, I was shocked to see that Liz had posted a job opening in Administration very similar to my old one, after ending my job for a supposed lack of funds. While some of the duties were her old budgeting tasks, the rest appeared to be my old duties, including project management and updating of my Master Plan. The person chosen, I found out, was a woman. The administration staff was now 100 percent female. Nice guys never seem to finish first in the city. It's not because they're nice. It's because they're guys. That was the last straw. Discrimination is against the law. It was time to stand up and fight back.

The next step was to file a discrimination claim with the Denver office of the Equal Employment Opportunity Commission. At first, the EEOC offered mediation to resolve the dispute, which usually means they thought a claim had some merit, and the city agreed to participate. But once I hired an attorney to represent me, the city's attorney withdrew and vowed to fight me in court. It's a long story, but the evidence of discrimination against men was considerable. Using data obtained from the city under Colorado's Open Records law, I discovered that the city's 520 management employees were more than 60 percent female. Out of twenty two departments, sixteen of them were greater than 50 percent female, but only six departments were greater than 50 percent male.

Yet Frank Bruno signed an official "diversity plan" that lumped "people of color" (who were rare, and for whom I believe extra consideration was appropriate) and women (who already had the majority of management jobs) as protected class groups. It ordered supervisors to "portray the city as an equal-opportunity employer by pictorially including people of color and females in city publications."[57] It also ordered that, "Advertisements for employment will be included in newspapers and broadcast media which target diverse and female populations..." and orders the human resources staff to, "Establish and maintain effective working relationships with representatives of diverse community groups and various women's organizations so that they may assist in referring qualified applicants for employment." White males need not apply.

Elsewhere in the city, pockets of gender discrimination appeared in the data. The strangest was in public works, where the sixteen-member Administration staff was 88 percent female, but the rest of the public works department was 80 percent male.

The entire library staff was 82 percent female. Yet, the members of the library's small computer and maintenance staffs were all men. It was quite segregated. I was the only male on the seven-person Administration staff, and once I was ousted, I was replaced by a woman. It would appear that this Old Girls Club was not interested in diversity, they wanted exclusivity.

When I took over Sally McVey's job of managing the building construction project back in 1989, I was doing two jobs but was paid 17 percent less than Sally, and Marcelee refused to correct it. When I pointed out to the city manager one day after a meeting that they wouldn't dare pay a woman less if she took over a man's job, he agreed and gave me the raise at once. And still, Marcelee refused to make it retroactive.

There are other examples of this reverse-sexism. Carol Ellinghouse, Boulder's water resources coordinator,

57. Frank W. Bruno, "City of Boulder Policies and Procedures, Diversity Plan," updated 03/24/03.

was invited by Marcelee to attend one of our staff meetings to give a presentation about where our water comes from. After introducing Carol to the staff, Marcelee made a statement like, "I think it's wonderful that the city government has entrusted something as important as our water supply to a WOMAN." Carol looked offended, as some people on the staff rolled their eyes, or looked like they were thinking, "there she goes again."

When Boulder had an interim city manager named Christine Anderson (between Ron Secrest and Frank Bruno), she was also invited to a library staff meeting and was introduced by Marcelee. One of the first things out of Marcelee's mouth was a statement about how Boulder finally got a woman city manager, even if she was only an interim one. She expressed this as a great victory. Ms Anderson didn't seem comfortable with the distinction.

And in 2002, the city hired a new Parks & Recreation director, Jan Geden. For the first time ever, the majority of city department heads were now women. I was told that Marcelee celebrated that milestone by hosting a party just for the women department heads.

Of course, there was no more obvious and powerful symbol of the hostile work environment for men than the image of twenty one cut-off penises dangling from a rope.

To some of my friends in Boulder who just couldn't bring themselves to believe that such a politically correct city could discriminate, I liked to put it to them this way. Suppose the genders of everyone involved in this mess were reversed. An organization that is 82 percent male is headed by a man who appoints an almost all-male team to manage before he retires. The group looks at the seven-person Administration staff and decides to lay off the solitary female, later replacing her with another man. I ask, "Would that ever be allowed to happen in that paragon of political correctness, the City of Boulder?" Invariably, the responses have been, "No way." My only remaining option to right this wrong was the legal system.

Unfortunately, the realities of my taking them to court were daunting. Every large law firm in Boulder told me that the city was a client, and could not represent me because of conflicts of interest. So I consulted with independent attorneys in Boulder and Denver. I learned that it would take over $20,000 in costs and legal fees to get it to a judge, and I was told that Federal judges are throwing out up to 70 percent of labor law cases these days. One attorney said that judges dislike labor cases almost as much as prisoner's rights cases.

I couldn't afford to lose. And even if you go to trial and win, you still lose after retainers, deposition costs, contingency fees and taxes are deducted. And the city has all the time and money in the world to fight me, and they know that. Besides, a court settlement would mean that the Boulder taxpayers have to pay, not the people at fault, who would suffer no consequences at all. I couldn't live with that. Despite having spent thousands of dollars on attorneys, I passed on the litigation with great reluctance.

So, 2004 began with that new director in charge. I got the first sign that things were not going well early that year when an article appeared in the paper. The library commission was strongly opposed to the Patriot Act (as were most librarians across the country), which gave Federal investigators the power to search library patron records for evidence of terrorism, or anything they pleased, without the usual search warrant. I was opposed to that part of the Patriot Act myself, and believed that the requirement of a search warrant would prevent abuse of privacy without undue hampering of an investigation, without turning libraries into safe havens for terrorists. But John Ashcroft, the former Attorney General, denied that the Act had ever been used in a public library. Even though a searched library under this Act would be prohibited from telling anyone it happened, I tend to believe that word would get out anyway, given the way that rumors seemed to fly so freely among librarians, and no case ever came to light.

But this newspaper article said that the library commission wanted the Boulder city council to write a letter to Colorado's elected officials in Washington, opposing the renewal of the Patriot Act. Most of those officials in Washington were conservative Republicans, all of whom were sure to remember that Boulder's library was the one who wanted to ban the American flag after 9/11. Such a letter could have the opposite effect, making them more determined than ever to renew the Act. The council, perhaps weary of criticism for taking on national issues, declined to write such a letter.

The Boulder Public Library didn't stop there. They announced to the public that patron borrowing records would be purged from the computer systems as soon as books were returned, leaving no trace for investigators. This nod to patron privacy was favorably received in the local press. There's a big problem, however, that was unrevealed, until now. What patrons do on the internet there is not private at all.

Years earlier, the library had purchased "monitoring" software from Elron Software Corporation for the networked computers. I saw a thick printout of web addresses, with terminal locations and other data, in Marcelee's office one day, long before the flag incident. I was shocked that she would allow the computer people to pry into what web sites our library patrons were visiting. She said it was only to see how many pornographic sites were being viewed, and the quantity was less than they thought. I asked if they were also spying on what the staff was doing without informing them, and she emphatically said she would not allow the computer staff to do that.

But one of the computer technicians told me they were watching and tracking how many "hits" or downloads each staff member made on the internet. Not surprisingly, I was informed that Larry was #1. Even worse, they installed PC Now on the network to watch what patrons and staff were viewing on the computer screens in real time. Big brother was watching the patrons. Now, they may be quick to claim that they have never used the spyware they purchased to watch patrons. But isn't that exactly what Ashcroft was saying about the Patriot Act, that they had the capability but we just had to trust them that it was never used? Then why did they have it? One of my first duties as the new director would have been to order that software off the network for good. If you are going to criticize others for having the capability to disrespect library patron privacy, you'd better clean up your own house first.

I waited many months in the early part of 2004 for a finance job to be posted in the city's Open Space department, at a similar salary to my old job. Bruno's displaced employee policy was supposed to extend through 2004. The man who used to hold the job is now in Nevada, but recommended to the supervisor that I be hired for it. But it was filled by an outside candidate, and I was never even interviewed. The displaced policy was ignored again. When I asked human resources why, they said I had received "extra consideration" before declining to interview me, which meant nothing. It sounded like I had been blacklisted by the city, and had no future there.

It was about that same time when I came across an upsetting article about a legal case involving the downloading of child porn by a library official. It said that a former vice provost and director of libraries at the University of Pennsylvania, Paul Mosher, was caught by technicians with more than five thousand images of child porn on his office computer, paid for with his credit card. He pleaded guilty to sexual abuse of children, unlawfully using his computer to view child pornography, and unlawful use of a communication facility. It was reported that he accepted responsibility for his actions and that he "had begun intensive therapy since his arrest."[58] While he faced up to fourteen years in prison on the charges, incredibly, he received only seven years probation and a $5,000 fine.

In mid-2004, I interviewed Jonathan Sawyer at Freewave Technologies, who led that group of employees to paste plastic flags all over the library entrance on the morning that first letter to the editor appeared about banning the flag. He had an amusing follow-up story.

Months after the media attention had passed, his wife convinced him to attend a silent auction for the Boulder Valley Women's Health Center. This center was founded in 1973 as the Boulder Valley Clinic, the first abortion clinic in the state. The Sawyers were quite surprised to see a familiar set of objects up for bid, a pair of the famous Susanne Walker ceramic dildos. His wife suggested placing a low bid on them just for fun, so he did. He explained that they didn't really want them, and expected more bids. To his surprise, no one else placed a bid, and they were the winners. I asked, "So what did you do with them?" He replied, "Oh, we *threw them away.*" He could be in trouble for that. Half of Boulder will be mad that he threw away *art*, while the other half (or possibly the same half) will be upset that they weren't properly recycled. Since they are ceramic, they may outlast the surrounding garbage in the landfill, and perhaps

58. "Mosher, Ex-Penn Library Director, Gets Probation," *Library Journal*, American Library Association, March 12, 2004.

some future archeologist will uncover them and wonder what role they played in our civilization.

Just after my layoff, I met with a friend at the Trident coffee shop and bookstore east of the Pearl Street Mall. He was the one who told me about Marcelee getting that personal letter of mine from the laser printer and how she showed it to him as proof that I had done this terrible thing to her. He said that she was convincing at the time, but that he found my story to be more credible. He quoted Marcelee as saying that she was glad my windowless office was located one floor down where she didn't have to look at me and that, "If I could, I'd move Chris to the darkest corner of the basement." He said she also questioned my politics, and said, "None of this would have happened if it hadn't been for Chris Power." I was shocked. He said she was too smart to take any action against me right away. It sounded to me like she had to have someone besides herself to blame for the big flag flap. Hearing this became a major reason for my decision to write this book.

In my research, I came across an article in *American Libraries* where Marcelee appeared to have refined her bizarre story of what happened. Here is an excerpt:

> BPL Director Marcelee Gralapp told *American Libraries* that it was never really a question of refusing to display the American flag. "There's already a flag outside the building and eight or 10 flags between the library and city hall and a flag in every meeting room—probably more flags than any institution in town." She said the flag proposed by a staff member was 8-by-10 feet, practically "as tall as a two-story building," and "people would have had to brush it aside to get through the door." She said it was also a simple matter of "flag etiquette."

Flags are supposed to be flown from poles, she said, and not hung from rafters and in people's faces.[59]

OK, time for a reality check. It certainly was a question of refusing to display the flag. There were no flags inside or outside the main entrance, in any meeting rooms, the auditorium, or anywhere else in the library until *after* the media got the story. Those ten outdoor flags, as I previously explained, were on the other side of Boulder Creek and far away from the proposed location. The flag was, of course, 10' × 15' in size. A two-story building only ten feet high, or even fifteen, would hardly meet code. I told her in that afternoon meeting that I had checked with the reference librarians about flag etiquette, and that hanging a flag vertically inside a building was permitted. And neither the large size of the flag, nor the ten existing flags on poles over on Canyon Boulevard, was mentioned by Marcelee in that meeting as reasons for not hanging a flag in the coneoid. The only reason given to me for rethinking her approval that day was America's foreign policies, despised by Larry and his South Americans.

Further research proved that my flag display proposal was perfectly proper. The Flag Code of the United States says, "When the flag is suspended across a corridor or lobby in a building with only one main entrance, it should be suspended vertically with the union of the flag to the observer's left upon entering. If there are entrances in more than two directions, the union should be to the east."[60] That entrance had doors facing north, south, and east.

As for this preposterous notion that the flag would

59. "Flag Flap Leads to Phallus Furor in Boulder," *American Libraries*, The American Library Association, January, 2002, 26.
60. The Flag Code, Title 4, U. S. Code, Ch. 1, Sec. 7, par. "o," revised and adopted 106th Cong., October 25, 1999.

hang in people's faces, or have to be brushed aside, please allow me to dispel that once and for all.

That glass coneoid over the entrance is big. Really big. I took out our construction drawings and measured before I wrote that first email to Marcelee proposing a 10' × 15' flag. So I went back to check my calculations. Could I have been so far off, and the flag really was too big?

No way. According to the architect's drawing, the top of the coneoid was forty one feet, one and one-quarter inch above the inside floor. The round base of the glass structure, sitting eleven feet above the floor, was thirty six feet, nine and one-eighth inches across, and even though it narrowed toward the top, there was plenty of room for a ten foot wide flag. I made a copy of the drawing and made a to-scale American flag as an overlay. In the proposed orientation facing north and south, the bottom of the hanging flag would have been a full twenty FEET from the ground. That space could have accommodated an even larger flag, but I saw no reason to do that. I just wanted it to be big enough to be recognizable from outside and from a distance.

On the facing page is that drawing, with a photo of me holding the folded flag, also sized to the same scale.

There you have it, the actual size of the flag in the proper context, with the union facing east. I had this checked for accuracy by one of the original architects, who said the flag would have fit just fine, and that I had sized it correctly. Even an NBA basketball star would not have been able to jump up to reach the bottom of that flag, much less have to "brush it aside." Nor was it true that "people would literally have to lift up the flag to walk in the door."

But this "too big" myth persisted. While speaking to another person on the staff one day about the flag flap, just before my layoff, an elderly volunteer in the room,

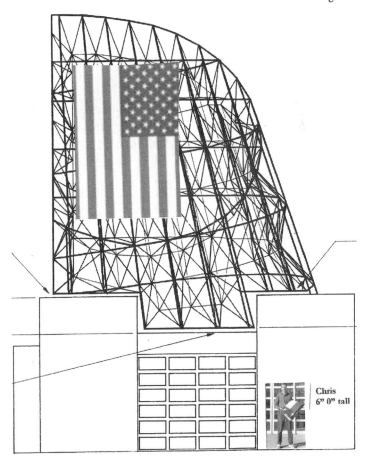

who must have been eavesdropping, chimed in. He declared, in a raspy voice, "That flag was so big, you would have had to push it aside to get in the building." I chose not to argue with him, but realized that Marcelee and the others had succeeded in manipulating the press and the public to believe something that was totally untrue. It was Marcelee's version of weapons of mass destruction, told over and over again until people believed it. I really want people to know the *truth*. It was not too big at all, and would have been a beautiful and thoughtful display.

She concluded her *American Libraries* interview as follows:

> Asked what she has learned from the flag and exhibits controversy, Gralapp told AL that the incivility of the criticism she received was frightening. "We've gotten 5,000 e-mails, and 4,995 of them were incredible; very few of them said anything nice. In the name of patriotism, we can be horrible to people."[61]

Indeed.

61. Ibid.

13

Bob Rowan, the "Dildo Bandito," waving to honking
cars on Canyon Boulevard. (Photo: Joe Pezillo)

Final Thoughts

When I was growing up, the introduction to each episode of *Superman* on TV mentioned his dedication to "Truth, Justice, and the American Way." I don't think Superman would ever want to fly into Boulder, since all three seemed to be in short supply in this case. Besides, he might get entangled in a clothesline full of dildos.

I knew it was important to set the record straight on this sordid episode when someone pointed out to me comments posted on a website about the University of Nebraska football team in 2005. It was a discussion about sexual harassment charges being made against the athletic department at the University of Colorado ("CU") in Boulder. Now that you know the real story behind the flag, this shows you how far off people can be with their information after the passage of time.

The first unnamed poster wrote:

> Every aspect of that city [Boulder] is just weird, everything is ass backwards. Here's a story for 'ya. A buddy I work with graduated from CU and said during the whole 9/11 aftermath some students started hanging American flags in the library. Hoffman [Elizabeth, former CU President] made the students take the flags down because she said it was not fair for the minorities from the Middle East on campus to have to look at the flags. Instead she has the students put up balloons in the shape of penis's to prove a point that "men" are the cause of all this.

Ha! Not even close. Balloons? Elizabeth Hoffman was getting a bum rap. A Boulder writer then attempted to clarify things, but didn't quite get it right either:

> What really occurred is two separate incidents not having anything to do with CU. Around 9/11, some citizens tried to enter the city library and hang a giant US flag in the lobby. The librarian at the time refused for a myriad of reasons, one of which was that there was no good spot to hang the giant flag. She did note, however, that on the 10 flagpoles surrounding the sidewalk outside, there were 10 US flags. The other incident was an art display at the city library that occurred pre-9/11. The display was artwork by women who had been victims of domestic violence. One of the displays included papier-mache painted penises. Yes, there was public outcry, as there should have been, con-

sidering the proximity to the children's section. The penises were removed.[62]

They certainly were. I hope this book can help clarify the truth behind this strange but important story.

In April, 2005, I was riding a chairlift at the nearby Eldora Ski Area on their closing day. A long-time resident of Boulder was on board, and I asked if he remembered the flag banning and art hanging incident. Not only did he remember, he said that he still refuses to set foot in that library because of it, and refuses to allow his five-year-old daughter to use it. He told me that they go to Longmont or Broomfield's libraries instead. It is important to point out to those of you who don't live here that not everyone in Boulder fits the far left stereotypes. There are many Boulderites who were just as outraged as most everyone else by this.

To summarize, after more than fifteen years of accomplishments and positive reviews in my employment at the Boulder Public Library, I suggest one day that we put up an American flag after 9/11 as a show of national unity, sympathy for the terrorist's victims, and a celebration of America's freedoms. It gets approved, and then turned down for a shocking reason. Penis display goes up. The press notices it all, and total chaos results. When the dust settles, I find myself an outcast, demoted, denied promotion, and the only member of the staff to be laid off from an institution I used to truly love. My seniority, pension contributions, health insurance, vacations, all gone. No immediate job prospects elsewhere. While this hardly compares to the scores of men and women who have lost their lives throughout history defending the American flag and what it stands for, I can assure you that the prolonged suffering has been considerable.

62. http://www.*HuskerPedia.com* March 17, 2005. Used with permission.

Meanwhile, Marcelee retires to her near-six-figure pension. Liz Abbott, the budget analyst who reportedly favored Marcelee's decision to ban the display of that flag, becomes the director in a process that can most kindly be described as having a greater than arms length stench.

I have lunches and coffees with many retired and current staff, most of whom say I am greatly missed, and/or that I was "really screwed." I asked one former library manager if there might have been some other reason for my incredibly harsh treatment, and she replied with great certainty, "It was the flag."

So, the question remains, why did Marcelee allow all of this to happen? She had so many opportunities to prevent this from becoming such a public relations disaster. She might have realized that there really is a difference between politics, which carries some legitimate concerns about objectivity in a library, and patriotism, which absolutely does not. She could have asked me to buy a smaller flag, or she could have said no to the flag at the outset, and that would have been the end of it. After telling me that Larry was upset about the idea, she could have compromised by telling him it would only be up for a few weeks, then quietly taken down. A simple sign below the flag could have stated that it was there out of respect for the people who died on 9/11, eliminating any implied support for going to war. She could have put the dildo exhibit on hold, or denied it from the start as inappropriate for children, or at least hung them behind solid screens with warning signs. And when the reporter called, she could have come up with plenty of ideas to satisfy him that there was no story, such as promising to put a smaller flag on a pole instead, but she didn't. She had to bring the question of objectivity and offense into the interview. And when the whole flag/dildo/Bandito story was going full tilt, she could have borrowed a lesson from that honorable librarian in Florida and issued an apology to anyone who was offended, but she did not, remaining defiant to the end.

If I had known sooner who was responsible for leaking this story to that reporter, I might have fended off this witch-hunt and attack on my reputation. I might very well have become the new director of the Boulder Public Library. Liz would still be there, doing the budgets. It could have been a happy ending.

After Liz began work as Marcelee's replacement and I was laid off on the *same day*, Marcelee told the *Daily Camera*, "I am very pleased."[63] She never once picked up the phone to call me since that day, which, as the librarians would say, "speaks volumes." Our relationship was over.

The current city manager, Frank Bruno, also bears responsibility in this matter. I believe he violated city policies twice, first for going outside to hire a headhunter to fill the director job before considering a displaced candidate himself as the policy demanded, and second, when questioned about it, disallowing the standard administrative grievance hearing for management employees because he didn't want anyone questioning his decisions. He also had a hand in perpetuating the discriminatory atmosphere against men.

I have reluctantly returned to the Boulder Public Library a few times at night, but only to gather research for this book from the microfilmed newspaper archives that are not available anywhere else. It's just too painful to go in there. When you walk into the main entrance toward the children's area, you have to pass a huge sign with the inscription, "Marcelee Gralapp Children's Library." Can you imagine that? I believe a more appropriate naming

<hr>

63. Greg Avery, "Boulder Appoints Head for Library," *Daily Camera*, December 19, 2001.

would have been the Judith Volc Children's Library, after Judy's many years of service as the director of that department. Or better yet, leave it unnamed. It belongs to the taxpayers.

My own future remains very uncertain. I continue to ski as much as I can in season. As I tell people, "If my life continues to go downhill fast, I might as well do it on skis." Or, "In Colorado, when the going gets tough, the tough go skiing." It beats therapy.

I also try to hold onto my sense of humor during my unemployment. One of my nuttier ideas, if nothing else pans out, is to produce a reality TV show for Bravo. I'd take a group of corporate executives and each week give them someone who has worked for some branch of government for his or her entire career. The challenge would be to get the bureaucrat retrained to function in a for-profit corporation. I'd call it, "Real World Eye for the Bureaucrat Guy," or something like that. Trouble is, I'm not sure it's possible.

So, now you know the real, ugly story of what actually went on during and after that unbelievable flag and dildo debacle. I wish that I had a happier ending to offer, but that's the trouble with true stories. Perhaps the positive result is that I live in a country where I have a constitutionally protected right to speak out about this without these government officials tossing me into jail.

The City of Boulder government used to treat its people very well in the past, and losing a job there was very rare, often the result of some kind of criminal activity. Now the welfare of Boulder's prairie dogs and pigeons is handled with greater interest and compassion. I'm certain that the city officials will be very busy crafting their spin on this story to make it go away, but I would take it with a large dose of skepticism. They will probably blame the budget situation, but don't believe it.

The reality is that the only library staff person they chose to terminate, out of about one hundred and fourteen employees, was me, the guy who suggested the post-9/11 American flag display. Was there a connection? You've read the story, you be the judge.

One sad, personal loss is a change in the way I feel about the American Flag. Where I once looked up and only saw a proud symbol of our country and our freedoms, I now just have a reminder of, well, all of this. Perhaps more time will heal these wounds. Despite my education and ambitions, the American dream hasn't exactly worked out for me in a material sense. But I hold onto my belief that in America, all kinds of things are possible, and that something good will come out of this. I would encourage all Americans to never take our freedoms for granted, no matter what your political views, and to be more aggressive about standing up against those who find our flag offensive. If I can do it, so can you.

Long may IT wave.

— Cast of Characters —

(Listed in the order they appeared in the story)

Christopher (Chris) Power—Former project manager on the library administration staff, who proposed the American flag display, and the author of this book.

Sally McVey—Original manager of the library building project, who hired Mr. Power and resigned after the architect selection process was completed.

Marcelee Gralapp—Former director of the Boulder Public Library, who gained national attention with her comments about refusing to display an American flag in the library after the events of September 11, 2001.

David Knapp—Former assistant city manager of Boulder, charged with the oversight of the library building project.

Eugene Aubry—An out-of-state architect selected to assist with the design of the downtown library building.

James Piper—Boulder city manager during the architect selection process.

Tech Logic Corporation—The Minnesota-based library systems company that designed and installed the robotic bookdrop at the main library.

Arthur Power—The author's father, who once worked on the ninety fourth floor of the World Trade Center.

Priscilla Hudson—The main library's branch manager.

Mark Koschade—The library's maintenance supervisor.

Larry—Pseudonym for the former library employee who objected to the flag display for political reasons.

Elizabeth (Liz) Abbott—Former library budget analyst, head of the interim Library Management Team, and eventual choice for the new director.

Ron Secrist—Boulder city manager during the flag and dildo episodes.

Greg Avery—A reporter for the Boulder *Daily Camera* who conducted the first interview with Marcelee where she raised her objection to displaying an American flag.

Jonathan Sawyer—Chief technology officer of Freewave Technologies, Inc. of Boulder, who led a group of protestors who taped flags to the library entrance.

Peter Boyles—Host of a morning talk show on Denver's KHOW radio, and "Colorado Inside Out" on KBDI-TV, a Denver PBS affiliate.

Steve—Owner of a cleaning and maintenance company who had a contract to provide custodial services to the library.

Bob Dickie—Marketing director, Tech Logic Corporation.

Donna Gartenmann—Staff liaison for the Boulder Arts Commission.

Susanne Walker—The artist and former University of Colorado student who created the dildo display.

Karen Ripley—Cultural program director at the Boulder Public Library in charge of art exhibits.

Anne Tapp—Director of the Boulder County Safehouse, a women's shelter.

Jann Scott—Host of a local cable access television program.

Kathy Hoeth—Library director at Florida Gulf Coast University, who also banned patriotic symbols from her library after 9/11, but reversed the decision and apologized.

Bob Rowan—The contractor who stole the dildos from the library, naming himself "El Dildo Bandito."

Mark Beckner—Boulder police chief during the flag and dildo episodes.

Frank W. Bruno—City manager during the library director recruitment process.

The Headhunter—The California recruiter hired to conduct the director search.

Will Toor—Former Boulder mayor during the flag and dildo episodes.

Tom Tancredo—U. S. Representative from Colorado, who sponsored a bill to deny federal funding to institutions that ban patriotic displays.

Jana Peterson—Spokesperson for the City of Boulder during the flag and dildo episodes.

Doug Lamborn—Colorado State Senator from Colorado Springs, who introduced a bill protecting the right to display American flags in tax-supported properties.

Paul Danish—Former Boulder city council member and Boulder county commissioner.

Mike Rosen—Columnist at the *Rocky Mountain News*.

Susan Honstein—Former human resources official at the City of Boulder, in charge of the director recruitment process.

Don Wrege—Lyricist who performed parody songs for Denver radio stations.

Ray Ingraham—Head of the library's computer services staff, and member of the management team.

Judy Volc—Former long time head of the children's room at the Boulder Public Library.

Hazel Cowan—The elderly volunteer who used to read to children, and leaked the news of the flag banning to her neighbor.

Sparky the Firedog—The Boulder fire department person in a Dalmatian costume who used to appear with Hazel during the children's story hour.

Steve Millard—Editorial page editor of the *Daily Camera*.

Roy Wallace—Interim director of human resources for the City of Boulder during the investigation of the recruitment process.

Elizabeth Hoffman—Former president of the University of Colorado.

Paul Mosher—Former vice provost and director of libraries at the University of Pennsylvania convicted of using his office computer to download child pornography.

To contact the author, order additional copies for your patriotic friends and family members, and to check for the latest news on this topic, visit the official internet site: www.longmaytheywave.com

ORDER FORM

Internet:
Visit www.longmaytheywave.com

Telephone:
Call this toll-free number: **1-888-548-7279**
Have your credit card ready.

Mail:
Send this form with your check, money order or credit card
information to:
Long May They Wave
Picea Press
P.O. Box 401
Boulder, CO 80306

*Quantity:*_____ at $14.95 each   Subtotal:_____

Shipping and handling:
$5.00 Priority Mail for first book,
$2.00 for each additional book.   Shipping:_____

Sales Tax (8.16% for Colorado addresses only): Tax:_____

                                                  Order Total:_____

Ship To:
Name:_____
Address: _____
City, State, Zip:_____

Credit Card payments:
☐ Visa   ☐ Master Card
Card Number:_____
Expiration Date:_____
Name on Card: _____

Billing Address (if different):
Name:_____
Address: _____
City, State, Zip:_____